INTROD...

This book gives a good deal of info... is neither a dictionary nor a formal gui... ...y way comprehensive. Instead, it is a light-hearted look at some ...ly personal favourite Scots words and I hope you will take a ramble through them.

Some of the words included are too common to omit even if had wanted to. These include such stalwarts of the Scots language as **couthie, douce, dour** and **dreich**. So common are they that they are likely to have reached a non-Scots audience while, of course, there is the ubiquitous adjective **wee** which Scots has donated to the world.

Then there are the words that I am particularly drawn to because no other word will suffice in that context. They somehow manage to capture the very essence of the meaning being conveyed and are quite simply untranslatable by any corresponding English word. The Scots language is rich in such words and I don't know how English copes without them

Such words include **swither** which means to be completely undecided about which course of action to take and to keep changing your mind. **Trauchled,** used to refer to someone who is absolutely exhausted, harassed and well on the way to the end of their tether, is another example of the untranslatable as is the less well-known, but utterly irreplaceable, **carnaptious** meaning ill-tempered and irascible. Also falling into this untranslatable category is **in a dwam** an expression indicating that you are not paying any attention to the present situation because mentally you are somewhere else or are in a state of utter blankness. Here too is **snell,** a word that perfectly conveys the penetrating, piercing cold of a winter north wind, and **thirled,** a word indicating that someone is bound to someone or something by particularly strong bonds of loyalty, duty, affection, or even habit.

Some thoughts of a rural childhood came to mind and reminded me of such favourite words as **bike** meaning a wasps' nest, **skelf** meaning splinter, **pawkies**, meaning mittens and **happit** meaning well wrapped up to keep out the cold. Then there is the great school no-no, **clype,** to tell tales. Somewhat unusually for a childhood memory the word **guddle** came to mind. This means to catch fish with your hands by tickling it on its underbelly. I never tried this illegal practice but an elderly male neighbour was a past master at it.

Then I have included some words that are particularly charming to the ear, as well as being useful. **Fernietickle**, translating a freckle is one of these. Another is **stravaig**, to roam at will and at your leisure. This is a good word to think of if you fancy a walk in the hills but are chained to the computer for the rest of the day.

Scots is rich in words used as insults and I have included a generous helping of these. So you will find the nouns **bauchle**, **nyaff** and **sumph** and the adjectives **shauchlin**, **shilpit** and **donnert** in this category. Should you be so unwise as to use these indiscriminately you may well find yourself in the middle of a **stramash** or **stooshie**, a row or uproar.

The book is easy to use. No specialist knowledge is required and no special instructions are necessary, except perhaps a mention that when a word appears in an article in bold type it indicates that there is a separate article on this word. The articles include the modern meaning of the word and often some historical ones. Where the pronunciation of a particular word is not obvious or straightforward I have given a simple guide as to how it is pronounced. Many of the articles include example phrases or sentences showing how the particular word is, or was, used. This feature makes the words come alive in a way that definitions on their own cannot.

Many of the words included have alternative spellings and some have quite a few of these. This is because Scots, unlike English, has no standard spelling scheme. This gives rise to the fact that one word may have several variant forms and it is sometimes difficult to find the word that you are looking for. This has happened to me. I once spent ages trying to locate a word that I had heard frequently in my childhood. The word was **snasters**, meaning cakes and pastries and other sweet things forbidden by most diets. I eventually unearthed it under **snashters** but finding it took some persistence.

As I said at the beginning of this introduction, this book is not at all comprehensive in its coverage. My apologies if I have omitted any of your particular favourites. Come to think of it, I may even have omitted some of my own. Whether you are taking a trip down memory lane, seeking more information on your Scottish heritage or Scottish culture generally or acquainting yourself with the Scots language for the first time, there is nothing else that I need to tell you about the book except 'Enjoy!'

- A -

AULD

Auld is the Scots equivalent of the English word *old* and it is often used in much the same contexts. For example, the expression old clothes translates as *auld claes*, old friends as *auld freens*, old house as *auld hoose* and so on.

However, *auld* has some uses that *old* does not have. *Auld* is often used to describe relationships. A grandfather can be referred to as *auld daddy* or *auld faither* and a grandmother as *auld mither*. One generation back a great-grandfather can be known as *auld granfaither* and the female equivalent as *auld granmither*.

An *auld uncle* is not necessarily an old uncle, but a great uncle, his spouse being an *auld auntie*. An *auld son* is not a male who is stricken in years. Nor is it the equivalent of the colloquial, rather patronizing and now dated English expression, "old son". Instead, it is used to refer to the oldest son of a family. Similarly, *auld brither* can be used to apply to your oldest brother.

The term *auld yin* is unisex and can be applied to either of your parents. I have also heard it used it of a female spouse. When capitalized as *Auld Yin* it can be used to refer to the devil. This is only one of many *auld* words for this creature from hell.

We have *Auld Clootie, Auld Hornie, Auld Mahoun, Auld Nick, Auld Saunders, Auld Spunkie* and several others to refer to the devil. Another of the devil's nicknames is *Auld Enemy*, but this can also be applied to England in recognition of the hostility and often open warfare that raged between the two countries for hundreds of years. Even nowadays the expression is sometimes mentioned at times of football or rugby matches between Scotland and England.

Scotland had friends as well as enemies. For a long time the closest of these was France and this friendship gave rise to the expression the *Auld Alliance*. The friendly links between France and Scotland so named began in the thirteenth century when both countries regarded England as a common enemy. Later they were much strengthened by the French

Favourite Scots Words

connections of Mary Queen of Scots. You sometimes still hear the expression when France is playing England in an international match and Scots are cheering on the French.

Auld is often associated with time and dates. The last night of the year, now mostly known as Scots *Hogmanay* or perhaps by the more anglicized version, New Year's Eve or the American version New Years, was once most commonly known as *Auld Year's Nicht*. *Auld Year's Day* is, as you would expect, the last day of the year. More difficult to figure out is *Auld Day* or *Aul Day*. This was once frequently used to refer to the day after a major celebration, such as a wedding, a ball, a feast, etc. It was apparently a day devoted to recovery from the excesses of the day before, a day when little work was done, although more than a little alcohol might be consumed-- a large hair of the dog perhaps.

Auld is encountered by a great many people outside Scotland because of its appearance in the internationally known song *Auld Lang Syne*. Sung at the end of various forms of celebrations, the song was written by Robert Burns to a well-known traditional tune. *Lang syne* means literally long since and so *auld lang syne* refers to the days of long ago. A word of warning. When singing this song remember that the initial letter is pronounced like the s in "sink" not like the z in "zinc".

Burns described the town of Ayr as *Auld Ayr* in his poem *Tam o Shanter* while Edinburgh was often referred to, and sometimes still is, as *Auld Reekie* because of all the smoke which once issued from its chimneys. *Auld* has another connection with chimneys because *auld wife* can mean a rotating chimney cowl as well as an old woman.

Auld wife can also be used to describe a fussy, pernickety, gossipy man, as in "He's a right *auld wife*." The meaning of *auld man* is more difficult to guess except in its literal meaning. Figuratively it means the same, unchanged, as in "I hadn't seen Jock for years, but he was still the *auld man*."

Someone who has a great deal of experience of something can be said to be an *auld used hand*. Someone who is *auld in the horn* is old and less fit, physically or mentally than formerly. It happens to us all!

- B -

BAIRN (*see under* **WEAN**)

BAUCHLE

In general, traditional Scots do not go in much for compliments. *No bad* is often the highest form of praise that leaves their lips. On the other hand, the Scots language is rich in words that can be used as insults. Such a word is *bauchle*.

As an insult directed at a person, *bauchle* was originally distinctly ageist and was used to refer to someone who was considered to be old, worn out and generally useless, well past their sell-by date, in fact. It went on to mean an untidy or shabby person or a clumsy person. When referring to a piece of work it was used to mean a botched job.

Then it came to be used as a general term of contempt for a person. Anyone you do not care for or anyone who has annoyed you in some way can be a *bauchle*. The first element of bauchle is pronounced in much the same way as "loch" and the word has various alternative spellings, mainly *bachle*.

As a noun a *bauchle* was originally an old shoe or slipper, especially one that was so worn and so out of shape that the wearer had no choice but to shuffle along. Presumably it was thought that the only people who shuffle along are old and generally past it.

Bauchle can also be a verb. Indeed *bauchle* was first recorded in Scots as a verb meaning to disgrace, discredit or to denounce someone publicly. It went on to mean to treat someone contemptuously or to cause them trouble or damage. If this damage was to a young woman, *bauchle* could mean to jilt.

Then the association with shoes and feet kicked in with reference to the verb meanings. *Bauchle* came to mean to wear shoes out of shape or to shamble or shuffle, as in worn-down or ill-fitting shoes. It also took to meaning to distort or spoil things other than shoes.

The origin of the word *bauchle* is unknown. It is possible that it has some connection with the Scots adjective *bauch*, meaning, among other things, in poor or weak condition. This, in turn, may perhaps be from Old Norse, *bagr*, awkward or clumsy. Etymology is sometimes an inexact science. Later the noun *bauchle* came to be used occasionally of a shoe in general, not just an old and worn one. Presumably a pair of designer killer heels could be described as *bauchles*, although the wearer undoubtedly would not thank you for the description.

BESOM

Scots is not lacking in ways of indicating our disapproval or contempt for others. Many of the nouns that fall into this category are either unisex or used mainly of men. However, there are exceptions to this and one of these is *besom*. When applied to a person these days, a *besom* is almost invariably female.

As is the case with many Scots words, *besom* has had various alternative spellings through the years. Some of these, which include *bisom*, *bissum*, *boosum*, *bizzom* and *bizzum*, more closely reflect the pronunciation of the word, because *besom* is pronounced not as the modern spelling suggests, but as *biz-zum* with the stress on the first syllable.

Besom carries a range of meanings. It was originally sometimes used of a woman whose morals were rather questionable and sometimes of a woman who was a bit of a slattern when it came to standards of hygiene. Nowadays, *besom* can be applied to a woman or girl whose attitude and behaviour we find unacceptable, to one who has annoyed us greatly, or just to one whom we thoroughly dislike. However, there can be a lighter note to *besom* and it can also be applied humorously or fondly to a mischievous child.

Besom is not always used of women. It can also be used to apply to an inanimate object, when it means *broom*, not the plant with yellow flowers, but a brush used for sweeping. The brush meaning of *besom* also appears in English, but there it usually applies to a rudimentary sweeping brush made from a bundle of twigs tied to a stick, the stick being known as a *besom-stick* or a *besom-shank*. In Scots, *besom* can also take this meaning, but it can refer also to a more sophisticated model of broom.

Besom is likely to be Germanic in origin, having come into Scots from Old English. The broom meaning of *besom* came first and the derogatory term for a woman probably arose from the associated idea of someone wielding a broom. Somebody such as a maidservant, whose job was sweeping up would be considered to be very low in status. The meaning went downhill after that.

A house that showed signs of being well-swept (or in these days well-hoovered) and was generally tidy could be described as *besom-ticht*, *ticht* being Scots for tight.

Rather confusingly, a house that was described as *besom-clean* left something to be desired in the cleanliness stakes. The floors might be swept, but not washed, and dust might be lurking elsewhere. I know that look.

Figuratively, *besom* can be applied to anything thick and bushy. It is particularly appropriate when applied to hair. I am familiar with that look, too, particularly on a bad hair day.

BIDIE-IN

I was reading an article about the rights of cohabitees the other day and could not help thinking what a clumsy, clinical and unattractive word *cohabitee* is. Not so the Scots word *bidie-in* which means much the same as *cohabitee*. What is a *cohabitee* or a *bidie-in*? They both refer to someone who is living with someone in a sexual relationship but who is not married to that person.

Bidie-in comes from the north-east of Scotland and was more or less restricted to that area for a long time, but things changed in the late 1970s and early 1980s. *Bidie-in* unexpectedly gained a degree of prominence not only in Scotland, but also in the rest of Britain.

At that time more and more people were choosing to live together, rather than get married. Some language experts became obsessed with finding a word to describe the person with whom someone was living in an unmarried state.

Lover was considered to be too racy and *partner* was originally set aside because of its associations with business. Some strange alternatives were put forward. One of these was *significant other* which went on to mean a person of importance or influence in someone's life. The strangest was *POSSLQ,* short for "persons of the opposite sex sharing living quarters". I kid you not, this was seriously considered. Fortunately it did not last.

Bidie-in popped up in the media coverage as a possible contender. It failed to win universal support, perhaps because it sounds too homely and cosy for sophisticated society. The word comes from the verb *bide* meaning either to stay somewhere temporarily or to live permanently in a place, to reside. It is closely related to the word *abide*, both having their roots in Old English.

What happened to *bidie-in*? After its brief spell of fame it returned to relative obscurity. More Scots from a wider area used it than before, but it faded from the UK scene. It, like the other suggested words, lost out to the word *partner*. Apparently its business connections did not matter after all. No surprise there, then.

BIKE

It is funny how mention of one word can trigger a whole series of memories. One such word is *bike*. I am not referring either to a bicycle or to a motorbike, but to the Scots word *bike* meaning a wasps' nest.

Mention of *bike*, also spelt *byke*, and pronounced like the shortened form of bicycle, for me conjures up memories of a rural childhood. In one of these memories my brother and I were aimlessly throwing stones at a strange big lump high up on the trunk of a tree. Well, it was decades before computer games and we had to make our own entertainment somehow!

Suddenly the lump burst into life and hundreds of angry winged creatures flew out. Now bike can refer to a wild bees' nest as well as a wasps' nest. I am not sure which this one was and we certainly did not stay around to find out. We were not budding entomologists and the swarm of insects looked distinctly dangerous. Bike can also be used of an ants' nests but that was beyond our knowledge and it was an unlikely nesting place for the average ant.

Looking back, some lines from Burns's *Tam o' Shanter* were particularly appropriate to the situation:

> *As bees bizz out wi angry fyke,*
>
> *When plundering herds assail their byke.*

We were not herds (shepherds) and we were not actually plundering, but the reaction of the bees or the wasps was the same.

Bike was once used to refer to a haystack or cornstack. It retained its association with insects, however, because such a stack was in the shape of a beehive. The word *bike*, which can also be used as a verb referring to bees swarming, is known to have been in use since the 15th century, but it is of unknown origin.

Bike can be used in association with humans as well as insects of various sorts. It could be used of a human dwelling or a kind of habitation, but it was more usually used to refer to a crowd or swarm of people. In this respect it has something in common with the word **hoachin**. Perhaps we could refer to a *bike* of tourists.

BLETHER

Eavesdropping on the conversations of fellow bus passengers is often a good way to remind you of the richness of the Scots language. The other day I witnessed two elderly women who met by accident on the bus greeting each other with great enthusiasm. Said one, "It's good to see you, Jean. We haven't had a *blether* for ages." They then proceeded to have an extended face-to-face *blether* for the rest of the journey while others chattered on their mobiles.

In this sense the Scots word *blether*, pronounced to rhyme with "tether", means a chat, often a long chat with a good deal of juicy gossip thrown in. For example you might say that many people who join a book group do so to have a good *blether* over a glass or two of wine rather than to take part in a great literary debate.

When applied to a person the noun *blether* means someone who is given to talking at too great length. You know the sort. They go wittering on and on long after the listener has ceased to listen. *Blether* can also be used to refer to someone who is apt to talk a lot of foolish nonsense. Often the two meanings meet together in one person.

The plural form of the noun, *blethers*, also takes up these themes of foolishness and long-windedness. It means foolish, nonsensical talk or long-drawn-out rambling in which there can be an element of bragging. *Bletheration* and *bletherie* are less well-known words for foolish talk

As an exclamation *Blethers!* means nonsense or rubbish. Should someone say something that you are deeply sceptical of or totally in disagreement with you can give expression to your reaction by exclaiming '*Blethers!* if you feel that a stronger expletive is inappropriate. As with a great many words, the noun *blether* has a corresponding verb. This was first recorded in Scots in the fifteenth century. Until the nineteenth century it was commonly used to mean to speak indistinctly or to stammer. More usually, its meaning is in line with the noun senses of *blether* and means to talk or chat, to indulge in foolish talk, or to go and on about something, often something unimportant. As is the case with the noun, the verb is also sometimes connected with boasting.

From the verb *blether* comes *bletherin*, used both as a noun and adjective to refer to foolish talk or verbosity, and, sometimes, to indistinct speech. Foolish talk and indistinct speech come together in one of the many Scots expressions for to be drunk. The phrase be *bletherin fou* (literally, full) means to be so drunk as to talk non-stop nonsense indistinctly.

Blether has an equivalent in English, the word *blather*, mostly found in informal or dialects contexts. As a verb this means to talk at length either without making much sense or to ramble on about things that are of little importance. As a noun it means long-winded talk of little meaning or importance.

Blether and *blather* are Old Norse in origin. They are connected with the Old Norse word *blathra* meaning nonsense or to speak indistinctly or inarticulately. An alternative form of *blather* is English *blither*, most commonly found as *blithering*, as in "a blithering idiot."

Blether has brought to us a word which, to me, is rather unattractive, but then it has rather an unattractive meaning. The word is *bletherskite*, with the alternative forms *bletherinskite*, *bletheranskite* and *bletherumskite*, and it is an insulting term used to refer to a person who talks a lot of nonsense.

The origin of the *skite* element is uncertain, although it has been suggested that this is derived from English *skate* the fish. Apparently this was once used as an insult and, certainly we still have the non-flattering term *cheapskate*.

We passed on the expression *bletherskite*, in the form *blatherskite*, not only to some English dialects but also to American English. I will not apologise for this in view of some of the words that America has passed on to us.

BODACH

Favourite Scots Words

When I was a child my father often used to refer to our neighbour as the *bodach*. I see that the pronunciation of this is given in some Scots dictionaries as *bode-ach*, the stress being on the first syllable and the *ch* being pronounced as the *ch* in "loch", rather than as the *ch* in "much".

My father, however, pronounced *bodach* with a *t* rather than a *d*, more like the pronunciation of the original Gaelic word from which the Scots word is derived. Like many Scots of that generation, he did not speak Gaelic, although both his parents did. It is one of those national disgraces that the language was not handed down in those days. My father did, however, have in his vocabulary more words of Gaelic origin than most.

Bodach in Scots means an old man. I have come across several references to the fact that the word is often used contemptuously. This was not the case with our neighbour. *Bodach* was applied to him by my father either in an entirely neutral way or even affectionately. For long enough I thought *bodach* was the old man's name, but, in fact, he was called "old Tom".

Bodach in another meaning can be used of either sex, sometimes appearing in the diminutive form *bodachan*. It means a small and unimportant, insignificant person. By very definition this is used rather contemptuously.

Bodach has a third meaning and in this sense it has spread its wings a bit. It means something supernatural such as a spectre or ghost, a *bodach glas* (grey or pale) being exceptionally scary because it supposedly usually makes an appearance as a herald to disaster or death.

Bodach is also used to refer to a bugbear or bogeyman with which children were threatenened to in an attempt to frighten them into behaving well. I would doubt if today's children, so used to horrifically scary aliens on television and films, would turn a hair at the thought of a *bodach*.

This meaning of *bodach* has gone beyond the boundaries of Scotland. It owes much of its success to Walter Scott's use of *bodach* in this sense. Being in Scott always represented a good entrée to the wider world for Scots words.

Then the spectral *bodach* was taken up by another, much later, literary figure. *The Bodachs* was the alternative title of Scottish children's writer Mollie Hunter's novel *The Walking Stones* (1970). Later still, the word *bodach* was adopted by American writer of suspense thrillers, Dean Koontz, in his tales of *Odd Thomas*.

Favourite Scots Words

Perhaps *bodach's* cleverest move was to get itself used in many Scottish place names. That way it is never going to be forgotten. One of the most famous of these is a Munro, *Am Bodach*, in Mamore Forest near Kinlochleven.

A possible contracted form of *bodach* is *bod*, meaning, like *bodach*, a person of small size, although the origin of *bod* is not certain. Formerly used as a nickname for a man of particularly small stature, *bod* is also found in English. In the English form *bod* is an informal word meaning either a person or the body. Sadly, it seems to be short for English *body* rather than for Scots *bodach*. Now that would have been a triumph.

BOORACH

A good example of a *boorach* is the kitchen of an enthusiastic but disorganized cook who leaves the kitchen sink and cooker hob piled high with every single pan and utensil in the place and the worktops a sea of half-spilt packets and bottles and dirty plates. In other words it means a state of great untidiness or confusion, a mess.

The Scots word *boorach* can also be applied to a scheme, often one involving several people, that might have started out as well-intentioned, but got horribly complicated and ended up in an almighty muddle. Several official schemes turn out to be *boorachs*.

Someone who is doing something in a very incompetent way can be said to be making a *boorach* of the task. For example, a novice knitter trying to knit a sweater might be said to be making a *boorach* of it, as might an inefficient person trying to device a complex timetable.

As is the case with many Scots words, *boorach* has several alternative forms, including *bourach* and the ch is pronounced in the same way as the ch of "loch". I had always assumed that the word was Gaelic in origin and was associated with the Gaelic word *burach*, to dig up. However, I see that an Old English connection has been suggested.

Boorach has several meanings. Before it came to mean a shambles, it meant a mound or a heap of something, such as stones or peat. Then it came to mean a crowd or group. It also took on the meaning of a particularly humble dwelling house and developed into a play house, often of sand, built by children. It has had an eventful life.

The word *boorach* was very familiar to me when I was a child, but I have not heard it for a long time. I hope it is still alive and well. I am sure that there are plenty of messy kitchens still around. I have one right here!

BOKE

Scotland's love affair with alcohol is well-known. Unfortunately the after-effects of this love affair are also well-known and one of the most unpleasant of these after-effects concerns the verb *boke*.

Boke means to vomit. Originally spelt *bock* and now often spelt *boak*, it is pronounced, as you would expect, to rhyme with "soak". In origin, it is onomatopoeic. If you have forgotten everything you ever learned about figures of speech at school, or were never taught any of them, this means that the word imitates the sound made by the action of the verb.

Boke, which originally meant belch and can mean retch, is a particularly good example of this. It suggests its meaning far more vividly than its English equivalents to vomit or be sick. Incidentally, the expression *be sick* has the distinct disadvantage that it is ambiguous. It can mean either to vomit or to be ill. For this reason, Americans often use the expression *be sick to your stomach* when they are referring to the vomiting sense.

Incidentally, Americans have an informal word for to vomit. The word is *barf*. In origin, it is also onomatopoeic and it is becoming increasingly popular in British English, mounting a challenge to *spew* and *puke*.

Boke can also be a noun. Thus, someone has to clean the *boke* off the bathroom floor after a post-binge incident. People can be left with tell-tale dried-in *boke* on their clothes, as a result of that sudden dash to the toilet after that one too many. *Boke* can also be used figuratively. If you want to describe something that you utterly disapprove of or find detestable, then *it gies (gives) me the boke*, as in "Her airs and graces fair gie me the boke (or boak)." ticks the right box.

If you want to emphasise your disapproval or dislike even further you can always turn to *it gies me the dry boke* (or *boak*). The *dry boke* (or *boak*) literally is that terrible stage further than vomiting when you have got rid of everything that was in your stomach and you are retching helplessly without tangible result.

BRAW

One of the most useful Scots words is *braw*. It is particularly productive because it can be used to indicate approval of just about anything or anyone. If you want to praise someone or something, or pay them a compliment, then *braw* is the word for you. In this respect it is a bit like the English word *nice*, except that *braw* is a notch or two higher on the complimentary scale than *nice* and sounds considerably more pleasant. The English word *great* is probably nearer the mark.

The word *braw* can be applied to the weather. If the sun is shining, the air is warmish and the sky is blue then it is *a braw* day. Of course, we do not get all that many such days in Scotland but, when we do, at least we have a word for them.

People can also be described as *braw*. This compliment often refers to their looks and nowadays it is more often used of women or children, as in *a braw lass* or *a braw bairn*.

Formerly, however, *braw* as applied in admiration to physical appearance was more used of men, as in *braw lad*. The expression *Braw Lad* is used in Galashiels to refer to the young man chosen annually by the people to represent the burgh at the Braw Lads' Gathering. His companion for the day is the *Braw Lass*, also elected by the townspeople.

Braw when referring to the male of the species meant handsome or of fine physique, the kind of physique that was necessary to do well in warfare. The ballad *The Bonny Earl of Murray* describes the earl as being *a braw gallant*.

It is fitting that *braw* had associations with warfare, because the word has connections with the word *brave* which indicates courage. Indeed, the word *brave* in English, like *braw* in Scots, once meant splendid or admirable as well as courageous, but these meanings are now archaic in English. Both *brave* and *braw* are derived from French.

Braw can also be used to indicate that someone is particularly well dressed on the day in question. Also, it can be used of a particularly impressive article of clothing, perhaps a brightly coloured summer dress suitable for *a braw* day. If you are dressed *in your braws* then you are attired in your very best clothes, the Scots equivalent of your Sunday best.

Braw can be used to describe anyone or anything that is particularly fine or excellent. So someone can be *a braw* piper, fiddler or singer. A particularly appetising meal can be *braw*, a musical performance can be *braw* and an especially picturesque view can be *braw*.

Occasionally, there can be a touch of irony in this use of *braw*, as when you comment that someone has got into *a braw mess*.

Money is something else that is often associated with *braw*. In this connection, *braw* usually means considerable or a lot and so a purchase such as a house or a flash car can be said to have " cost you a braw penny". Sometimes there is an underlying suggestion that the purchase was not a good idea. Time, too, has a *braw* connection. If you arrive somewhere *in braw time* you are in good time and can congratulate yourself on your punctuality.

Useful a word though *braw* is, there are those who never use it, even when expressing approval or admiration. They find *braw* far too fulsome and stick to *no bad* for their most extravagant form of praise.

BUNNET

An American friend was visiting Scotland recently and asked me to accompany her on a search for suitable gifts to take home to those left behind. One of the gifts she had in mind, she said, was a hat for a male relative.

To me, the male hat falls into two categories, the kind worn by the older sartorially elegant something in the city (and even they might have given it up) and, more commonly, the winter woolly headgear that often bears a distinct resemblance to a tea cosy. Since the American friend lives in the midwest, which can get extremely chilly in the winter, I assumed she was in pursuit of the cosy-type hat, probably one with earflaps.

But I was wrong. When we entered the first shop and she explained to the shop assistant what she wanted, the assistant brought a series of soft, flat, peaked caps. She called them tweed peaked caps. To me, they were *bunnets*.

The English equivalent of Scots *bunnet*, sometimes spelt *bunnit*, is *bonnet*. *Bonnet* and *bunnet* have their origins in the Old French word *bonet*, derived from the expression *chapel de bonet*, meaning a hat or cap made of *bonet*, a kind of material. *Bonet* is related to medieval Latin *abonnis*, headgear.

Favourite Scots Words

Bonnet was originally a unisex word. It could refer to any form of male or female headgear that lacked a brim. It was once frequently used to describe a woman's headgear of the variety that tied under the chin. However, a *bonnet* was also worn by the likes of Burns's Tam o' Shanter, who was said in the poem which bears his name to be "holding fast his gude blue *bonnet*."

Nowadays, the word *bonnet* is mostly found referring to the hinged cover for the engine at the front of a car – what the Americans call the hood – but it is also used to describe the headgear, of the tam o' shanter, or Bamoral type, worn as part of the dress uniform of some Scottish regiments.

Bunnets, however, are clearly still alive and well and living in gift shops, even although they may be called *caps*. Probably the nearest English equivalent to *bunnet* is the expression *cloth cap* which, like *bunnet*, has a soft top and stiffened peak. The *cloth cap* was once principally the headgear of male manual workers, while those further up the employment tree were wearing soft hats. Because of this, *cloth cap* acquired political connotations and became a kind of symbol of the working class.

The word *bunnet* does not seem to have achieved the political standing of *cloth cap*. It is true that *bunnets* are worn by male manual workers, although for decades they have also been worn by huntin', fishin', shootin' types on grouse moors and the like.

However, the fact that *bunnets* were associated with the working class is remembered in the expression *bunnet hustler*. This is a west of Scotland expression for a person, now well-off and comfortably ensconced in the ranks of the middle class, who is excessively proud of their working-class roots (which may or may not have existed) and acts accordingly. We have all met one of these, I am sure, often in the world of politics.

- C -

CARNAPTIOUS

The great thing about many Scots words is that they are much better at conveying their meaning than many English words. In many cases, their very sound suggests their area of meaning. Take *carnaptious,* for example. The word is pronounced with a kind of snarl and, fittingly, it is used to describe a very ill-tempered person who is prone to snarl at people, often for no good reason.

Carnaptious describes someone who is permanently angry and looking for a fight, rather than someone who has got out of the wrong side of the bed and is temporarily out of sorts. Apart from ill-tempered, English equivalents include bad-tempered, cross, irritable, irascible and grouchy. The closest equivalent is probably *cantankerous*, but even this is not in the same league as *carnaptious*.

A *carnaptious* person makes you feel that they will bite your head off as soon as look at you and, in fact, the word is likely to have associations with the verb *knap*, meaning, among other things, to bite or snap. For some reason *carnaptious* is often used of old people, but I am sure this is unfair and ageist. Surely there are some *carnaptious* young people about, though I doubt that they would admit to it.

A milder form of *carnaptious* is Scots *crabbit*. I tend to think of a *crabbit* person as being more passive than a *carnaptious* one – equally as irritable and as unpleasant to be around, but less likely to attack you with little or no provocation.

Crabbit is the equivalent of the English *crabbed* with the same meaning, but *crabbit* is more widespread in Scots than *crabbed* now is in English. Both *crabbit* and *crabbed* are linked to the crab. Apparently, crabs have long had a reputation for being easily annoyed because of their habit of holding up their pincers when they think they are being threatened.

We cannot really blame crabs for being *crabbit,* or even *carnaptious*. The thought of ending up on someone's dinner plate is excuse enough.

CHAP

In English *chap*, like bloke and guy, is mostly used to refer to a man. Now considered a bit old-fashioned, *chap* is either used neutrally, as in "There's a *chap* at the door." or used in an approving way, as in "He seemed a pleasant enough *chap*." We do not seem to have many nasty *chaps* around".

In Scots a *chap* at the door is usually not a person at all. It commonly means a knock at the door. This meaning of *chap* can also be a verb and so you might well hear someone *chappin* (=*chapping*) at your door. You might even hear someone *chappin* at the window.

Chap, the original form of which was *chop*, derived from Middle English, means to knock, strike or tap. People playing dominoes are said to be *chappin* when they cannot play. Sometimes they actually tap the table to indicate their inability to play; sometimes they just announce the fact.

A *chapper* most usually describes a thing used for striking or knocking, specifically a door knocker, though I suppose you could describe someone knocking at a door as a *chapper*. Certainly *chapper-up* was used to describe a person. In some parts of Scotland it referred to someone who was employed to go through the streets, banging on the doors of the workers to encourage them to get out of bed and go to work. This was, of course, before the days of alarm clocks, wake-up telephone calls and mobiles.

Not only doors and tables are associated with the verb to *chap*. Clocks, such as church clocks or grandfather clocks, are said to *chap* when they strike the hour or other division of time. On the culinary front, *chap* is associated with vegetables, particularly potatoes. To *chap* vegetables is to mash them. People who attend Burns Suppers, and there are legions of them, may well be familiar with the dish known as *chappit tatties* (mashed potatoes, now trendily known as mash) which accompanies haggis and *bashit neeps* (=mashed turnip).

There was originally a word *chap* in Scots which shared the English "man" meaning and they were both derived from *chapman*, a merchant or pedlar. In Scots this word developed the meaning of lover and it was sometimes applied to a woman. Watch out! A "*chap* at the door" can be a bit ambiguous.

CLYPE

The school is a long-established learning institution, but nowadays it seems ever-changing so that parents, and even more so grandparents, scarcely recognize it as the same institution which they attended. One thing, however, does not change. *Clyping* is still against the unofficial school moral code and swift retribution will be heaped by their peers on anyone who is so foolish as to *clype*.

Clype, pronounced to rhyme with "ripe" and having the alternative spelling *clipe*, is a Scots verb meaning to tell tales, in other words to tell a teacher about a piece of wrongdoing carried out by another pupil. For once, something is known about the origin of the word. *Clype* is related to the Old English word *cleopian*, meaning to name or call.

I am sure that we all have school-day memories of sitting in a classroom waiting for someone to own up to something considered wrong, while the teacher threatened that the whole class would be punished if the culprit was not identified. Often the whole class was punished unless the culprit reluctantly decided to confess. Still we did not *clype*.

We might all have known the identity of the culprit, but mass punishment was considered more acceptable than *clyping*. Was this the school equivalent of honour among thieves? Perhaps so, but just as likely is the fact that we were all scared of the wrongdoer.

Clype did not always carry the sense of getting someone into trouble by reporting what they had done. It once simply meant to relate or tell about something that had happened, whether the event was bad or good. Before that it meant to be exceptionally talkative, to gossip a lot.

Clype can also be a noun. Nowadays, it usually refers to someone who tells tales, but it once was commonly used to mean a tale, whether it was the kind of tale borne by a tale-bearer or just a story. It was also used to refer to a piece of gossip or even a lie.

A tale-bearer was once also known as a *clype-clash*. A more charming word for this, linguistically unrelated to *clype*, is *tellie-speirie*.

After we leave school we seem to leave the word *clype* behind us. There are still tale-bearers around, but we tend to call them different things according to the situation. For example, we have informers, squealers, grasses, whistle-blowers and investigative journalists.

Of these, *whistle-blower* is the most general, but the activities of a *whistle-blower*, unlike those of a *clype,* are sometimes actively encouraged rather than frowned upon. *Whistle-blowing* often involves an employee disclosing information about some form of malpractice or wrongdoing in an organization and it is sometimes officially known as *public interest disclosure.*

Who knows? Perhaps *clyping* will one day go the way of *whistle-blowing* and become acceptable and even actively encouraged.

COUTHIE

A friend was recently showing some foreign visitors round parts of northern Scotland and encountered the usual problem of finding somewhere to stay and eat out of season. She eventually found somewhere, commenting later "It was a bit *couthie*, but it was perfectly adequate and it had a great view of the loch."

Knowing her well, I deduced from her comment that the accommodation was a good deal less sophisticated and trendy than she would have liked. The house was probably furbished with multi-coloured, lavishly patterned carpets and wallpaper which would have offended her minimalist taste.

Couthie as used by her was clearly not intended as a compliment, but this critical use is a fairly recent development. *Couthie*, when used of places, originally meant cosy or comfortable, or generally pleasant and agreeable. Indeed, it often still does. "A *couthie* place with a view of a loch" might be some travellers' description of a perfect holiday location.

Couthie, which was a fairly late entrant into the Scots language, not making an appearance until the early eighteenth century, can also be used of people. A *couthie* host, for example, is one who is exceptionally friendly and sociable. If he or she extends a *couthie* welcome then it is a very warm one indeed. You are fortunate if one of your friends can rightly be described as *couthie* when you are in times of trouble because it means that you have a sympathetic audience.

How did a word which is descriptive of such sterling qualities come to be used critically? Well, from being used as synonym for comfortable, it came to be a synonym for homely. Now a place described as *homely* is often regarded as somewhere warm, friendly and comfortable, but it can also be regarded as somewhere very simple or unpretentious and ordinary. Incidentally, the Americans go one further and sometimes use the word homely as a synonym for unattractive.

We now live in a world which is nothing if not pretentious. Being homely or ordinary is rarely regarded as an asset. In such an environment it is hardly surprising that *couthie* has lost some of its high-ground status and is now sometimes used critically.

Couthie may not always have the complimentary associations it once had, but it certainly has not reached the depths that the word *uncouth* has. Yet they are related, both having their origins in Old English *cuth,* meaning known or familiar, which is derived from Old English *cunnan*, to know. *Couthie* is also related to Old Scots *couth,* meaning known or familiar.

Couthie's change in meaning sometimes causes a degree of ambiguity. Is the reviewer describing folk music played by a local amateur band as *couthie* being complimentary or critical? I fear the latter is usually the case.

Crabbit *see under* **Carnaptious.**

- D -

DINGER

What is most likely to make you *go your dinger*? No, this is not a rude question, and I certainly do not want any rude answers. In Scots to *go your dinger* is to become extremely angry. This does not relate to just any old anger, certainly not to the kind of anger that leaves you silently fuming in the corner.

No, if you *go your dinger* you give maximum vent to your anger, going on and on about the cause of your anger in a most vocal way. For example you will frequently find parents *going their dinger* when their offspring have transgressed in some way. You can also still find some people *going their dinger* about things that upset them in the correspondence columns of newspapers.

Go your dinger is not necessarily connected with rage. It can also be used to mean to do something very actively and enthusiastically. At a party you might refer to young people still *going their dinger* on the dance floor when older and less energetic mortals have long crept home to their beds. Or you might refer to the band at the same party *going their dinger* as they play their various musical instruments with great gusto.

Dinger, the first syllable of which rhymes with "ring", is a relatively recent word, but it has its origins in a much older word. It is derived from the verb *ding* meaning to beat or strike. This was in use in the fourteenth century and is thought to be derived from Old Norse *dengja* to beat, thrash or hammer. *Ding* went on to acquire other meanings such as knock, push, shove or drive.

Once, if you *dinged oot* someone you replaced them in another person's affections. In modern parlance you would be the cause of someone being dumped. If you *dinged yirsel* you let something vex or annoy you (presumably before *going your dinger*).

Should you try to *ding* something into someone you try hard and persistently to get some kind of information into their thick head. If a blow to the head *dings you donnert* it makes you mentally confused. Talking of blows to the head, *ding* can also act as a noun meaning a blow, knock, push or nudge.

The verb *ding* can also mean to defeat, beat, get the better of, wear out or tire out. It is to be found in the exclamation *that dings dinty!* meaning that beats everything, that is the absolute limit or words to that effect.

Some of you may be familiar with the saying "Facts are chiels (young men, fellows) that winna ding", a quotation from Robert Burns's poem *Dream* meaning that facts cannot be denied. Of course, many politicians, and others, have tried to disprove this saying.

Ding also has associations with the weather. When used of rain, snow or hail it means to fall heavily and continuously. A *ding-on* was a heavily fall of any of these, but the syllables were reversed and became *onding*, now the usual term. There's nothing like a relentless series of *ondings* to get the populace *going their dingers* about the climate.

Donnert *see under* **Sumph.**

DOUCE

Douce, with the alternative spelling *douse*, is pronounced to rhyme with "loose". Like many words in both English and Scots, it is derived from French, having its roots in the Old French word *dous*, modern form *doux*, feminine form *douce*. This in turn comes from Latin *dulcis*.

Dulcis and *doux/douce* both mean sweet and, when it first came into Scots in the 16th century, *douce* also meant sweet, in the sense of soft, gentle or pleasant. This meaning has survived to the present day and you can refer to "*douce* breezes on a balmy day". Well, you can if you are living in fairly warm climes. In Scotland violent gale-force winds rather than *douce* breezes can be the norm.

Douce in this sense can also be used of people or their way of life. For example, you might talk of a neighbour who was "a *douce* old woman that everybody liked". However, when used with reference to people nowadays, *douce* is now more likely to mean sedate, sober or respectable. For example, you might say "For years most of the young people have left to go and study or work in the city and, for the most part, the remaining community is a bit *douce* and rather elderly."

Favourite Scots Words

This use of *douce* can be complimentary or neutral, but *douce* can be used in a critical or condemnatory way. It depends on your point of view and attitude to life. If you are rather a wild child who loves to paint the town a vivid shade of red then you might well use the word *douce* critically of someone who likes to stay at home reading a book, and even occasionally going to church.

Douce can also be used to mean neat, tidy or comfortable. This meaning can apply to people and in this context it can also mean rather stout. It can also apply to things. Thus, you can describe someone's house as *douce* if the owner has spent time hovering, dusting and decluttering it. I rather think my house does not wholly qualify for the epithet.

Nowadays *douce* is probably most commonly used of places which are noted for their quietness, sedateness and even lack of progress. Again, this use can reflect a critical attitude. It is not everyone's idea of a dream holiday to spend it in a *douce* seaside resort. They would regard it as being stuck in a boring backwater.

I mentioned above that *douce* is derived from French, but it is not one of those Auld Alliance words which came straight to Scots from France without stopping off in English. Such words include *ashet*, meaning a large plate for serving meat and the like, and derived from French *assiette*, a plate.

No, *douce* did make an appearance in English, but it became obsolete and now just appears occasionally in the north of England. The English were probably glad to get rid of it. They never did have much fondness for the French.

DOUR

Many Scots nowadays are stay-at-homes at heart, not venturing forth much to other countries except for the odd business trip, weekend break, or the almost mandatory two-week beach laze. It seems recently that even their holiday travel has been, curtailed thanks to the recession and cutbacks, and they are becoming staycationers (a very unattractive word).

Favourite Scots Words

Many Scots words also stay at home. Indeed they are even less likely to settle elsewhere than the people. However, just occasionally we find that one of these words has slipped off to foreign parts and has been adopted by the natives there. These parts often include the United States, Canada, or Australia. Sometimes they include the area south of Watford. And it is to that area of southern England that the Scots word *dour* has spread. You will even find it in English dictionaries.

Dour is pronounced to rhyme with "moor", although in the south I have sometimes heard it pronounced to rhyme with "glower", doubtless a happy combination of words if you are a budding poet in melancholic mood. *Dour* has been known in Scots since the fourteenth century, but it is of uncertain origin. However, it seems likely that it has connections with Latin *durus*, hard.

The word *dour* in England and elsewhere is often used with reference to Scots people, and not in a complimentary way. However enlightened modern civilization has supposedly begun, racial stereotyping is still alive and well, and living in a great many places. A common racial stereotype is the "dour Scot". The drunken Scot is an even more common racial stereotype, but let us stick to one thing at a time.

Dour is an adjective of many parts but, as far the stereotyped "dour Scot" is concerned, it means humourless and sullen. Smiles are rarely seen on the face of such a one. However, there are Scots who would say that this alleged lack of humour is a misinterpretation. Humour is not lacking at all, but takes the form of a subtle, dry wit, that is beyond the comprehension and appreciation of those who prefer their humour in more obvious, laugh-a-minute, form.

Dour can also mean obstinate, stubborn or unyielding. If you are the kind of person who refuses to allow people to railroad you into things, then you will see yourself as a resolute person sticking to your guns, while others may describe you as *dour*.

Not only people can be described as *dour*. A task that is exceptionally difficult to carry out can also be so described. Thus an arduous job such as digging the garden or clearing the driveway after a very heavy snowstorm can be dubbed *dour*.

Favourite Scots Words

If someone or someone is reluctant or slow to do something they can be referred to as *dour*. This use can cover a whole range of situations. School pupils can be described as *dour* if they are reluctant to settle down to their studies or if they have difficulty in learning. Fish can be described as *dour* if they have the sense to keep a low underwater profile and refuse to take the bait. A fire can be described as *dour* if it is slow to burn and does not produce instant warming flames.

Weather gets everywhere and it is not surprising that *dour* can also be applied to it. *Dour* skies are dark and threatening and a *dour* day is a gloomy, bleak one, the sort that makes us long for one that is simply **dreich**.

DREICH

In Scotland November has more than its fair share of celebratory events. It catches the tail end of Hallowe'en, it rejoices in the Guy Fawkes festivities which seem to go on throughout the entire month and it ends with St Andrew's Night. Of course, there is a sadness to November in that contains Remembrance Day, but, for the most part, November is a party month.

Surely, therefore, we should think of November as a cheery month. Not so. Quite a few people regard November as the very epitome of misery and a great many Scots would describe it as *dreich*. The ch is pronounced as in Scots "loch" or German *ach*.

Dreich has several meanings when applied to weather, including wet, dull, gloomy, dismal, dreary, miserable or any combination of these. It sums up November to a T, probably because we tend to concentrate on the wet, bleak weather characteristic of November, rather than on the revelries.

The word *dreich* has its origins in Middle English and, indeed, once was a feature of English as well as Scots. It is now obsolete in general English, although, like several other Scots words, it is still to be found in Northern England. *Dreich*, however, is unusual in that people living in the leafy suburbs of the south have been known to use it. Usually, Scots words do not reach that far. Should we regard this as a success story for the Scots language?

The original basic meaning of *dreich* was protracted or long-drawn-out. From this developed the meanings tedious or wearisome. People have traditionally associated both of these meanings with sermons. In the days when most people still went to church, those ministers who liked the sound of their own voices would deliver very long and uninteresting orations from the pulpit. These sermons were frequently dubbed *dreich*. No wonder some people introduced a happy-clappy element to services.

Of course, not only sermons can be *dreich*. Anything lengthy that bores you stiff can also be *dreich*. Obviously this includes something written or spoken, such as lectures, after-dinner speeches, reports, plays, etc, but it can also be extended to such things as journeys, tasks, football matches etc.

People can also be *dreich*, and in more than one sense. Boring, dull, lack-lustre people can be described as *dreich*. As you might expect, depressed, gloomy people can also be so described. However, *dreich* people can also be slow or unpunctual. Specifically, they may be slow in paying their bills, leaving their creditors less than happy. You have to think twice before you call someone *dreich*.

Incidentally, if someone is *dreich a drawin* or *dreich in drawing* it means that they are very slow when it comes to making a decision. Such a delayed decision was often related to a romantic relationship. Someone who was *dreich in drawing* showed a distinct reluctance to propose marriage even after long years. Nowadays, we refer to such a person as a commitment-phobe.

A *dreich* task, as I have mentioned, can be a boring, long-lasting one. It can also mean a difficult or puzzling one or one that requires close attention. As you can see there is more to *dreich* than meets the eye. It goes from dry sermon to wet day with much in between.

DROOKIT

Drookit is Scots for absolutely drenched. It fittingly describes that miserable state when, despite the protection of supposedly waterproof clothing and umbrellas, you are wet through to your very bones, and even to your very souls. You really have to live in a wet climate to appreciate the appropriateness of the word.

Favourite Scots Words

Compared with other Scots words, *drookit* is still in fairly common use and I think its use could increase in the future. This is because the nature of the Scottish rainfall seems to have changed recently. We are well used to precipitation of all sorts from a gentle drizzle to relentless heavy rain, but the kind of rain we sometimes get now more resembles a monsoon. It is heavier than any previous torrents and seems to come out of nowhere. Perhaps this is the Scottish version of climate change. Whatever the reason, *drookit* is the perfect word to describe its drenching effect on us.

Drookit, which is sometimes spelt *droukit*, is pronounced *drook-it* with the first element of the word rhyming with "look". It is derived from the verb *drook* or *drouk*, to drench, soak or steep. The origin of this is uncertain, although it might have some connection with Old Norse *drukna*, to be drowned.

Drookit is usually used to refer to people or, perhaps to vegetation, such as trees. The verb *drook* or *drouk*, however, was originally also used to mean to soak something, for example oatmeal, bran or dried beans as well as to drench people.

Drook is sometimes associated with moisture other than rain and the phrase *in a drook (or drouck) of sweat* was once quite common. Perhaps some of you might know it—or still use it. Another phrase associated with *drook* which I have just discovered is *drookit stour*. Stour is dust and so *drookit stour* is wet dust or mud. This is sometimes referred to as *glaur*.

The verb *drook* has given us the noun *drookin* as well as the adjective *drookit*. Getting *a right drookin* is a regular part of the Scottish summer experience, as visitors will find out. But it will not detract from their enjoyment.

DROUTHY

Drouthy, also commonly spelt *droothy* and pronounced like that, whatever the spelling, means thirsty. Thus, if you have been on a long walk on a hot day and omitted to take a bottle of water with you, you could well end up *drouthy*.

However, the thirst involved in *drouthy* is usually a desire for strong drink rather than for water or other beverage. When Burns wrote in his well-known narrative poem of *Tam o Shanter*:

> *And at his elbow Souter Johnny,*

His ancient, trusty, drouthy crony

he was not suggesting that Tam's friend Souter Johnny was in need of a glass of water or orange juice. No, Souter Johnny was in dire need of some ale and whisky. Burns makes it clear that Tam and Johnny were regular drinking companions and regularly drank too much.

If someone is described as *drouthy* it often carries the implication that the person is permanently in need of strong drink. In other words, they are addicted to alcohol, or to put it more euphemistically, they have a drink problem.

Originally, *drouthy* referred to the weather and meant dry or exceptionally dry. I seem to remember that we used occasionally to have *drouthy* summers, but recently these have largely disappeared. They still have these in the south of the UK, although not so called, but they have become part of the north/south divide, leaving us with several inches of rain while our southern neighbours complain of a drought.

Originally, *drought* meant simply dryness and it is etymologically connected with Scots *drouth*, from which *drouthy* is formed. Both *drought* and *drouth* have their roots in Old English *drugath*.

Drouth can mean a drought, but it can also refer to a drying breezy weather of the kind that is perfect for drying clothes. *Drouth* can also mean thirst. If you *have a great drouth on you* you can have need of a large glass of water or something alcoholic. People who regularly give in to such a *drouth* too often need to watch out. They may grow into *drouths*, in other words alcoholics. Eventually, they may end up literally dying for a drink.

DUNT

Some words are much better than others at suggesting their meaning. Scots has many such words, one of them being *dunt*. *Dunt* as a noun usually translates into English as a heavy *blow*, which just goes to show how superior the Scots language is in this respect.

Blow, whose origin is unknown, may be hard-hitting in meaning, but it sounds a bit of a lightweight in comparison with *dunt*. The English word *thump* is probably nearer the mark.

Favourite Scots Words

Dunt, which also appears in some Northern English dialects, first appeared in the Scots language in the sixteenth century. The origin is a bit uncertain, but it is likely to be imitative of the sound made by a heavy blow, especially a heavy, dull-sounding blow. Good old onomatopoeia in action again. *Dunt* is likely to have associations with English *dint* and Norwegian dialect *dunt*, a blow.

The noun *dunt* can be used in various contexts. A severe *dunt* to the head can render you unconscious and get you transported to hospital. The word *dunt* can apply to the wound caused by a heavy blow as well as to the blow itself. A severe *dunt* on the head might take a long time to heal.

If the person next to you at a lecture or some kind of performance is falling asleep you can give them a *dunt* with your elbow to wake them up. Many a recalcitrant machine springs into life after a good *dunt*. The careless driver behind you can give your car a substantial *dunt* if you have to stop suddenly when their attention is elsewhere.

Dunt can also be used to refer to the sound made by something heavy falling. Thus a big tree can fall with a *dunt* in a storm. *Dunt* can also refer to a quickened heartbeat, and, if you are very scared or anxious, you can be only too aware of these *dunts* in your chest.

The noun *dunt* can also be used figuratively. Thus, your confidence can take a bit of a *dunt* if you fail in some enterprise and your trust in someone can also take a *dunt* if a promise is not kept. If you *tak a dunt* generally your plans and hopes have received a major setback.

The word *dunt* is also used as a verb with meanings corresponding to those of the noun. So it can mean to beat or strike someone or something, as in to *dunt* someone with your fist or *dunt* someone's nose. It can mean to bump into something, as in to *dunt* a wall when you are reversing the car carelessly. The heart can *dunt* alarmingly in moments of fear.

Curiously enough, the expression *dunt oot* does not involve violence or blows. It is a non-aggressive expression meaning to thrash out the details of a misunderstanding or quarrel to try to settle or resolve it. You might have expected fisticuffs.

Dunt has several interesting phrases connected with it. There is *in a dunt*, meaning very rapidly. If something is *the verra* (very) *dunt* it is the very thing, just what is wanted. If you are told to *never let dunt*, you are being asked to keep your mouth shut about something. To *get the dunt* is to be

Favourite Scots Words

knocked out or, figuratively, to get the sack. Finally, there is the old proverb "Words are but wind, but *dunts* are the devil". How true.

DWAIBLY

Every now and then we can all feel a bit *dwaibly*. There are various reasons for this. We might be suffering from the effects of the common cold or even flu (and in many people's terminology these two are the same, especially when it comes to concocting a reason for taking a sickie from work). We might be recovering from an extended shopping trip, especially when the cold realization of what we have done to our wallet or credit card hits us. Or we might be enduring the pain of the morning after a boozy night out.

What is *dwaibly*? Those of you who have not encountered the word before will doubtless have come to the conclusion that to be *dwaibly* is not a happy state and you are quite correct. *Dwaibly* is Scots for weak, shaky or wobbly. It can be used to describe a general state of health (or rather lack of it), but it is often used specifically of the legs. When your legs are *dwaibly* it is best just to sit down or take to your bed in case you fall over.

Dwaibly comes from the adjective *dwaible*, which in one sense means much the same as *dwaibly*, weak or shaky. In another sense it is used to mean either pliant or flexible, and in yet another sense it means flabby.ike so many Scots words, *dwaible* has a number of alternative spellings including *dwabble*, *dweeble* and *dwobble*. I rather like *dwobble*. Somehow it sounds even weaker and shakier than *dwaible*. Perhaps that is just because it calls to mind thoughts of wobble.

Dwaible can also act as a noun. It is used to refer to a person who is weak or helpless, as a young child or an old frail person. However it can be used of someone who is in such a condition because they are over-tall – vertically challenged as PC-speak would have it – although, confusingly, this can also mean exceptionally small. Of course, exceptional tallness does not necessarily suggest weakness or helplessness. Think of powerful towering basketball players or American football players.

As a verb, *dwaible* means to totter along or to walk in a wobbly way. It could be used to describe the unsteady, ultra-cautious way that many older people adopt when walking on icy pavements. *Dwaibly* came from *dwaible*, but where did *dwaible* come from? Good question – and, as is so often the case in etymology, the answer is that the origin of the word is

31

uncertain. One suggestion is that *dwaible* was formed from *dwabbling*, an Old Scots word meaning feeble or unsteady.

Come to think of it, I am feeling a bit *dwaibly* myself. I had better go and have a lie-down.

DWAM

Many Scots words are so fit for purpose, as they say in modern parlance, that it is difficult to find an adequate English translation for them. Such a word is *dwam*, usually to be found in the phrase *in a dwam*.

Dwam in this sense is often translated as *daydream* but this strikes me as a bit too poetic for *dwam* and not accurate enough. A daydream suggests pleasant thoughts and fantasies indulged in while awake.

Dwam does not suggest anything so creative. If you are *in a dwam* you are not necessarily building castles in the air. Rather, the phrase suggests blankness. When you are *in a dwam* you may be thinking about something, not necessarily something pleasant, other than the subject in hand. However, you are just as likely to be thinking about nothing at all.

The other translation frequently given for *dwam* is stupor, but this is often defined as a state of near-unconsciousness and a *dwam* in the sense I am thinking of is nowhere as deep-seated as that. Furthermore, dictionaries frequently indicate that a stupor is often brought on by drugs or alcohol. Not so *dwam*. It does not necessarily have any connection with illegal substances, although the odd dram-induced *dwam* is not unknown.

Dwam, with the alternative spellings *dwalm* and *dwaum*, when it first came into being, was used to refer to a physical condition. Germanic in origin, it has associations with Old English *dwolma*, a state of confusion. As a verb it meant to faint or swoon or to become suddenly ill and also meant to decline in health. As a noun it meant a fainting fit or a sudden attack of illness. In this older sense the notion of stupor was more relevant.

So how should be *in a dwam* translate into English? Be in a reverie is another possibility but reverie raises much the same problem as daydream. Be in a state of abstraction is quite apt, but it is a bit of a mouthful. Staring into space and lost in thought both cover the situation quite well, but are not as concise nor as graphic as be in a dwam. I suggest you stick with *in a dwam* whether you are Scots or not.

- F -

FANKLE

It could be that some of you out there lead impeccably well-ordered, muddle-free lives. Congratulations to you, but most of us are not like that. From time to time we get into a *fankle*.

A *fankle* is a muddle or state of confusion. Such a state can arise in even the best-organized families, for example at holiday time. No matter how foolproof your forward-planning seems to be, no matter how many detailed lists you compile, no matter how many times you check passports and tickets, the adults in the household at least usually get into a *fankle* just before the journey begins.

The mind is most likely to get into a *fankle*, hopefully temporarily, when you are nervous. Having to speak in public is enough to set some people straight into a *fankle*, sometimes resulting in them losing the place, literally and figuratively, halfway through the speech.

It is common for business affairs to get into a *fankle*. People who start their own businesses with great enthusiasm and talent, but with little aptitude for numbers or accounts, can soon end up with their financial affairs in a *fankle*. The remedy is to call in an expensive accountant or the administrator.

Originally, it was something more concrete than business affairs that got into a *fankle*. Inexperienced knitters, for example, can get their wool so tangled up that it ends up in a *fankle*. Amateur anglers can get their fishing lines in a similar state.

Fankle can also act as a verb meaning tangle, although this use is now less common. If you are tossing and turning restlessly at night you can get the bedclothes so *fankled* up that you can scarcely get out from under them. Children, especially those new to the art of skipping, can get their skipping ropes *fankled* and, figuratively, income tax affairs can get *fankled*, although this is unwise.

The verb *fankle* originally meant to trap or catch in a snare. In origin, *fankle* comes from *fank* meaning, as a noun, a coil of rope, a noose or a tangle and, as a verb, to tangle or twist or to catch in snare, net or trap. This is not to be confused with *fank* meaning a sheepfold which is derived from Gaelic *fang*.

I hope you are having a *fankle*-free day. If you are not, do not worry. You will not be alone.

FANTOOSH

There's much to be said for taking the bus in the city even if you do have a car. Apart from the obvious advantages, such as avoiding extortionate parking fees, you can salve the greener part of your conscience by helping to save the planet and you can indulge in a bit of eavesdropping. I mean listening in to real head-to-head conversations and not to the clichéd mobile conversation which begins, "I'm on the bus…"

Overheard bus conversations produce some real gems. The other day I was diverted to hear an elderly woman say in an impeccable Morningside accent: "He's married again already and his second wife is much more *fantoosh* than Jean ever was." Jean appeared to be the not-very-long-deceased wife.

Fantoosh, pronounced as it is spelt, and with the emphasis on the second syllable, is a Scots word which, when used of a person, means over-dressed or ultra-fashionable, bordering on the flashy. It seems to be mostly used of women and an over-dressed woman can be called a *fantoosh* or described as *fantooshed*. However, I am sure that there are bound to be some *fantoosh* men around nowadays when so much money is spent on men's grooming.

Fantoosh, meaning ostentatious or pretentious, can also be used of inanimate objects and can refer to a wide range of things. Weddings tend to bring out the *fantoosh* in people. Many people tend to go way over the top when it comes to their big day and produce everything from *fantoosh* invitations to *fantoosh* floral displays to *fantoosh* wedding favours to *fantoosh* bridal hairstyles to *fantoosh* wedding cakes. Wedding guests often add to the general air of *fantoosherie* with their *fantoosh* hats.

The word *fantoosh*, whether referring to the animate or the inanimate, is usually used as a term of criticism or disapproval. Thus, the woman in the bus who so described the late Jean's replacement was certainly not delivering a compliment.

It is strange, given the disapproval that is traditionally attached to *fantoosh*, that several modern shops or businesses, from restaurants to flower shops to hat shops to flooring specialists, use the word as a name to trade under. Perhaps the owners of the businesses just like the sound of the word and have never investigated its darker side. The *Scottish National Dictionary* suggests an interesting and unusual origin for *fantoosh*. It says that the word appears to have been coined during World War I, having been influenced by the obsolete English slang word *fanty-sheen* meaning, as a noun, a marionette or, as an adjective, showy or fanciful. This is thought to have originated from the Italian word *fantoccino*, meaning a puppet, which is related to French *fantoche*, also meaning a puppet.

Other commentators on Scots suggest that *fantoosh* has come straight from the French word.

Reverting to my comments on overheard bus conversations, I have found that these are not infrequently a good source of Scots words. This is partly because many day-time bus passengers in Scotland are of the age to be in possession of a free bus pass. Their very age makes them more likely to be in possession of a vocabulary that, at best, is rich in Scots words and, at least, often contains a smattering of them.

FERNIETICKLE

Fernietickle, pronounced as it is spelt and sometimes spelt with a hyphen or as two words, is Scots for freckle. *Fernietickle*, also known as *ferntickle*, is derived from Middle English *farntikylle* and is thought to take its name from the fact that a freckle resembles a brown fern spore, not a particularly attractive origin. The "tickle" part is probably from *tickle* meaning a small part or grain.

Fernietickles are not always regarded as an attractive feature. A scarcely discernible light dusting of them is thought to be all very well, but, when they overlap and join up with each other, *fernietickles* seem larger and much more obvious. It has to be said that *fernietickles*, however small or large, are usually much more obvious to the bearers of these than to people who are viewing them on the skin of others.

Nowadays, *fernietickled* people (I was going to say particularly women, but given the money spent on men's cosmetics, this is perhaps no longer true) often go to great lengths to find some kind of bleaching cream that promises to cure them of what they regard as a skin problem. Older suggested remedies included the use of vinegar, lemon juice or buttermilk.

It was also hoped by some *fernietickled* people that the traditional custom of washing the face with early-morning dew on the first of May, thought to be a general beauty-enhancer, would remove their *fernietickles*. People who are subject to a covering of freckles find that these get more prolific in the sun. To avoid this they can also just stay out of the sun, not a difficult task in the Scottish climate.

Some fond relatives try to relieve the concerns of young people who are wreathed in *fernietickles* by telling them that they should be pleased about their facial feature. Formerly they often went on to say that *fernietickles* were a sign that people exhibiting them were actually a form of chosen people. This was because the fairies (good fairies that is) had bestowed the *fernietickels* on them at birth.

Fernietickles are not usually seen on people with darker complexions, but are a particularly common feature of the fair Scottish skin. They are typically to be seen on the skin of red-haired people with such a skin, but dark-haired, fair-skinned Celts are also frequently *fernietickled*.

Incidentally, *fernietickled* is not restricted to skin. It can also be used of something, such as a story or comment, that is very often, probably too often, repeated. This is a much more attractive way of saying hackneyed, overworked or even clichéd.

FLIT

Some words are much better than others at conveying their range of meaning by their very sound. Such a word is modern English *flit*, as in small birds or butterflies flitting from tree to tree. Somehow the short word suggests both lightness and swiftness.

However, these qualities are rarely present in connection with the Scots word *flit*.

In Scots, the most common modern meaning of *flit* is to move house. Unlike the *flitting bird* or *butterfly*, the *flitting person* is likely to experience heaviness and a painful lack of speed if the furniture to be moved is a bit bulky.

A Scots *flitting* can be problematic. How did you ever get that cumbersome wardrobe up all those narrow stairs? More importantly, how will you ever get it down all those narrow stairs? Will you have to take out the window panes and lower the wardrobe down on ropes? Will it reach earth safely?

As to lack of speed, you are already on your third day of going through all those old business papers that were estimated to take two hours max. And those piles of newspapers and magazines with the potentially interesting articles that have accumulated over several years unread? Suddenly they make fascinating and urgent reading. And you have yet to clear the attic.

In order to be able to *flit*, as in move house, with lightness and swiftness, you really need to be a minimalist with hardly any furniture and certainly no clutter. Alternatively, you could be one of those compulsive *flitters* who never stay in one house long enough to unpack. Once they have the keys to a new property they are off checking estate agents' windows and internet sites to find their next home.

A *flitter*, as you might expect, is someone who *flits* in the house sense. The word, however, can also apply to a professional removal man or woman. Is that the answer, then? Call in the professionals and introduce some lightness and swiftness into the *flitting* process that way. Yes, if you are exceptionally lucky; no, if you are not. *Flitting*, like Christmas, is a major source of stress, whoever carries it out.

To *flit* in the house-moving sense was once commonly used in English as well as Scots, but it has died out in England, except for northern English dialects. *Flit*, derived from the Old Norse verb *flytja* meaning to transport, was originally used to mean to remove anything from one place to another, not just a family and their belongings. Specifically it was used to mean to move tethered animals to a new field to graze. It could also mean to depart, or even to depart this life and die.

Flit can also be a noun referring, like *flitting*, to the act of moving house. The traditional day for farm workers to leave one employer and move to another was known as *Flit Friday*. An old saying, however, advises that intending *flitters* should avoid Saturdays. The saying, *Saturday flit's a short sit*, means that Saturday *flitters* will not stay long in the next place, something compulsive *flitters* would doubtless welcome.

The expression *moonlight flit* has rather a romantic ring to it. It sounds as though it might, for example, refer to star-crossed lovers who are eloping. Alas, its meaning is much more prosaic. It means a house-moving that takes place suddenly at night in an attempt by the *flitter* to avoid paying debts. Given the present economic state of affairs, *moonlight flits* may well be on the increase.

Favourite Scots Words

FOOTER

There are some Scots words which are particularly useful because they are virtually untranslatable and *footer* falls into this category. *Footer*, pronounced as this spelling suggests and also spelt *fouter*, is usually translated into English as fiddle, potter or trifle.

Fiddle or potter, according to context, at least give an impression of what is meant, but not so the word trifle. You might trifle with someone's affections, but I doubt if you would *footer* with them.

The verb *footer* is frequently associated with children. They are likely to be told to stop *footerin* with an object, such as a pencil, when they are supposed to be giving their undivided attention to something that an adult is saying to them. Instead, they are constantly touching and turning over the said pencil — or other object — and frequently looking down at it. This can be described as fiddling but this somehow lacks character.

A particularly useful thing to *footer* with is one of this little figures made out of Lego. You can turn this over and over, take pieces off and put them back on again, all the while not listening to what an adult is saying. Do pass this piece of advice on to the children in the family if they have not yet discovered this skill for themselves .

To *footer* can also mean to act in rather an aimless way, often when you should be getting on with some specific job. In order to postpone the evil moment of actually embarking on the task, you drift around in a fairly relaxed fashion, doing a bit of this and a bit of that. People who work from home are particularly familiar with this kind of *footerin*. This style of *footer* is usually translated as potter, but it sounds better in the American English version, *putter*.

Footer can also be used as a noun. In one of its meanings it has the sense of someone who *footers* in either sense. It can, therefore, refer to someone who touches and turns something over and over again or to someone who roams aimlessly from minor task to minor task. Again, the word is often applied to children, wee *footers* as they are.

The noun *footer* can also be used of a task. The task in question is an awkward one, often involving working with extremely small parts, and requiring a degree of manual dexterity. As you grow older and fingers become arthritic, more and more tasks become *footers*. Even something as simple as putting batteries in the remote can become a bit of a *footer*.

Footer has given rise to the adjective *footerie*. As you might expect, a *footerie* task is a manual one that is awkward or difficult to do because it involves intricate work or small parts that are difficult to manoeuvre into position.

Footer appears to have a rather unusual French connection. It is thought to be associated with the Old French word *foutre*, which, in turn, comes from the Latin word *futuere*, meaning, of a man, to have sex with someone.

You might wonder whether we could accuse Nero of *footerin* while Rome burned. Alas, no. According to tradition, he was not literally twiddling his thumbs during the conflagration. He was playing on a lyre.

FORBY

Every English thesaurus lists quite a few synonyms for the adverb *besides*. These include also, too, as well, moreover, furthermore, what's more, in addition, additionally and over and above that. Some of these have Scots equivalents such as *tae* (too), as *weel* (as well) and *whit's mair* (what's more) but Scots can make a contribution to the list that is all of its own.

The word is *forby*, pronounced with the emphasis on the second syllable. Formed, as you might expect, from the words "for" and "by", forby has its origins in Middle English. It was formerly to be found in English as well as Scots, but now its use in English is confined to certain dialects. *Forby* has the alternative spelling *forbye*, which sometimes becomes *forbyes*, although this is now rather old-fashioned.

As indicated above, the adverb *forby* means in addition, as in "The weather forecast said it would be fine, but it was rainin and cauld (cold) forby." and as in "He injured baith (both) his arms in the accident and broke a leg forby."

Forby can also be a preposition with meanings corresponding to those of the adverb. Thus it means in addition to or as well as, as in "I kent (knew) a few there forby the hosts. *Forby* as a preposition can also mean except or apart from, as in "Forby the family, there were nae (no) mourners at the auld (old) man's funeral." and as in "We loved the place forby the weather."

Forby can also be used to mean let alone, much less when used in such constructions as "The flat's no big enough for the kids, forby guests." *Forby* as a preposition can also be used to mean compared with or relative to, as in in "The hooses (houses) on the estate were of average size, but minute

Favourite Scots Words

forby the laird's palatial place." *Forby* has some meanings that seem to have become more popular in Ulster Scots than they did in the home-made variety. Ulster Scots came into being when the Scots language was taken to Ulster in the early part of the 17th century by the large number of Scots who settled there under the Plantation policy of King James VI and I. By means of this policy of colonization of parts of Ireland the king hoped to quell the rebellious Irish.

Of these meanings of *forby* that became more common in Ulster one is its use as an intensifying adverb, meaning extraordinarily or unusually, as in "He was a huge, strong man, but he was forby gentle." The other is *forby* as used as an adjective meaning uncommon, extraordinary, unusually good, as in "It'd take a forby man to take on that task."

One more thing. Should you be described as being *forby yirsel* it means that you are out of your mind. It's a bit like being beside yourself, but even worse.

FYKIE

All of us have our likes and dislikes. Some of us, however, take things to extremes and we become too fussy, finicky or faddy. In Scots, people who are ultra difficult to please are described as *fykie,* which rhymes with "crikey". People can be *fykie* about many things in life, however trivial, but a lot of *fykieness*, or *fykerie*, centres on food. Long past are the days when everyone ate everything on their plate because there was nothing else to be had and the alternative was hunger.

The huge range of foods on offer has played into the hands of the potentially *fykie* and there are none so food *fykie* as children, especially with regard to anything green on a plate.

Fykie people were not originally finicky. The adjective was first applied to people who cannot or will not sit still. To be *fykie* was to be restless or fidgety. Then it developed its modern meaning. A *fykie* boss is difficult to please and fusses about what you might consider to be unimportant details, but *fykie* can also apply to the job the boss asks you to do. A *fykie* task is one that is difficult or wearisome to carry out for some reason . It is often one that requires a great deal of care or attention to detail.

Fykie is derived from the verb to *fyke* which has several meanings and which has its origin in the Old Norse word *fikjast*, to be eager or restless.

One of these meanings is to fidget or to move about restlessly whether from anxiety, excitement or boredom. Another is to be anxious or worried about something. Yet another means to exert yourself to an unusual extent or to take a great deal of trouble over something. Then there is the meaning which has most connection with the usual sense of *fykie*, to make a great fuss over something unimportant.

The verb *fyke* gave rise to the noun *fyke* which also has a range of meanings. These include a fit of restlessness, a fuss or commotion, and trouble or a source of annoyance. More in line with today's common meaning of *fykie*, the noun *fyke* can also mean a whim or fad, or an over-fussy person or a person who makes a great to-do over something of very little importance.

There we have it. Would you describe yourself as *fykie*? Probably not. You are probably just exceptionally discriminating and discerning.

- G -

GIRN

Children have the advantage over adults when it comes to expressing their dissatisfaction with life. They can have a foot-stamping tantrum, a good old screaming session or a fit of anguished sobbing in response to the most trivial thing. True, some people might look askance at the parent who is allowing this to occur, but an adult indulging in a similar display would probably be carted off to a psychiatric clinic. In Scotland, a child can go one better than all of the above and simply *girn*.

If you have ever been unfortunate enough to listen to a child *girning* you will know that to *girn* means to complain constantly in a high, one-note, drawn-out tone, whilst somehow managing to cry at the same time. It is usually translated into English as to "whine", but it definitely loses something in translation. Incidentally a *girning* child is quite a common sight—and sound—in supermarkets.

Not only children *girn* in Scotland. Adults also do so, but with a very slightly different meaning. *Girning* adults complain or grumble incessantly, but their grumbling usually lacks the high-pitched sound effects achieved by children that can drive parents mad. For example, a neighbour who goes on and on about people parking in front of their house without permission can be said to be *girning* adult-style. *Girn* originally had a physical meaning. It meant to show the teeth as a result of anger, pain, or exceptional physical effort and could also mean to grimace or snarl—not a pretty sight. It then went on to mean to show feelings, such as disapproval or dissatisfaction, by screwing up the face in this way. From there it was but a short step to the modern meaning of to grumble and from that it was an even shorter step to the *girning* child.

Just to confuse things, *girn* could also mean to show the teeth as a result not of anger, but of scorn or mirth. Someone *girning* could be sneering or grinning and this gets us to the origin of *girn*. *Girn*, which, like many Scots words, is also used in parts of northern England, was the same word as English *grin* until metathesis occurred. For those of you unfamiliar with this aspect of language, metathesis occurs when two letters or sounds change places. You also find it in English *griddle* and Scots *girdle*.

Just think. But for a mere switch of letters the *girning* child could have been a *grinning* child. What a difference this would have made to family life!

GLAIKIT

We all feel the need to direct an insult at someone occasionally to show that we are less than happy with them. Not infrequently the insult suggests that the person so addressed is slow-witted or foolish. In Scots one of the words commonly used to indicate this is *glaikit*, pronounced with the emphasis on the first syllable which rhymes with "take".

If you describe someone as *glaikit* you can mean that you consider them to be permanently lacking in any sense and that they are, quite frankly, stupid. On the other hand, the smartest people can be rightly accused of being *glaikit* if they are having a bad brain day or if their brain is not yet in gear. Temporarily, they are not very bright and are guilty of doing something which you think is foolish or senseless.

Glaikit can be used of foolish or irresponsible actions as well as foolish or irresponsible people. So you might comment when someone has just had their car stolen that it was a *glaikit* thing to do to leave the keys in the ignition.

Glaikit is also frequently used of facial expressions or physical appearance. If someone is standing still, with a blank look on their face, especially when they should be in proactive mode, someone may well say "Don't just stand there looking *glaikit*. Do something!" Someone dressed in full evening dress might feel that they look really *glaikit* getting on public transport in the middle of the afternoon, although such an action is necessary if they are to get to the appointed venue in time.

Formerly, *glaikit* meant playful or given to playing tricks or pranks. It could also mean flirtatious, although, not surprisingly, this was mostly used with reference to women. Real men do not flirt, do they? Deceitful was another common earlier meaning, although this appears to have been more unisex in its application.

The origin of *glaikit* is uncertain, although it is likely that it has connections with *glaik*, a verb of obscure origin meaning to look foolishly at or to trifle or flirt with. Also connected, and also of obscure origin, is the noun *glaik* meaning a stupid or irresponsible person, often, apparently and quite unfairly, used of the female of the species.

This noun was originally found only in the plural form *glaiks* and meant deception or trickery. If you *gie* (=give) *someone the glaiks* or *fling the glaiks in someone een* (=eyes) you are out to deceive or delude them. On the other hand, if you *get the glaiks* you are the one being deceived. Perhaps you have been a bit *glaikit* not to have sussed this out.

GLAMOUR

Many of the televised reports of the Oscars ceremony are as much concerned with what the rich and famous are wearing as with the identity of the winners and the losers. There for us all to see is the fact that Hollywood is still synonymous with *glamour*.

But what is this do with Scots? A great deal, because the word *glamour* has its origin in the Scots language. *Glamour* in Scots meant enchantment, magic or witchcraft. It also meant a spell, especially one that affected the eyesight of the recipient of the spell, as in *to cast the glamour ower the een* (=eyes). If this happened to you, your view of things became very different from the reality.

English has Sir Walter Scott to thank for its acquisition of the word *glamour*. Some of his work had quite a following in England and in a note to one of his narrative verses he explained the Scots word *glamour* in the sense of spell and how this spell was said to distort people's image of things. You can begin to see how we acquired the modern sense of *glamour*. *Casting the glamour ower the een* made people see things unrealistically. Acquiring modern *glamour* needs the help of cosmetics, designer labels and bling. So both senses of *glamour* have a deceptive quality.

There is something else unusual about *glamour*. It was originally a modified form of the word *grammar*. *Grammar* originally meant learning in general, rather than its modern sense, and it also referred to a knowledge of the occult or magic. Thus, *grammar* and *glamour* were both caught up in witchcraft.

In time both *glamour* and *grammar* discarded their associations with the occult and went their separate ways. The former became the friend of celebs everywhere. The latter used to be an essential part of education.

Glaur *see under* **Drookit**.

GOMEREL

Gomerel is Scots for a stupid or foolish person, or someone who – in the opinion of the user of the word – has behaved foolishly or unwisely. It is pronounced with the emphasis on the first syllable, which rhymes with "gone", and you can get a great deal of passion and venom into its rather guttural sound.

Gomerel is most commonly used as a noun, but it can also act as an adjective. The word will gladden the hearts of those who never quite mastered spelling, because it has several alternative forms, such as *gomeril*, *gomeral* and *gommerel*. It is virtually impossible to misspell it, although *gomerel* is the most usual modern form.

Gomerel has another meaning and a curious one at that. Occasionally it is used to describe a person whose lower front teeth stick out beyond the upper teeth when their mouth is closed. It would be ungracious, not to say untrue, to suggest that such a dental feature is typical of fools, and so this meaning is a bit unfair.

The word *gomerel* is likely to be the source of *gommy*, a word which is found in the west of Scotland and has the same meaning as *gomerel* in its sense of fool or stupid person. *Gommy* can also act as an adjective. Someone whose stupidity knows no bounds could be described as *a gommy eejit* (idiot), unless they are bigger than you are and you are within striking distance! *Gomerel* has its roots in the Scots verb *goam*. *Goam* can mean to look around rather vacantly in an unfocused way, as you might do if you get off a bus at the wrong stop in a strange place and have no idea where you are. Apparently animals, as well as humans, are prone to *goaming*.

Goam can also mean to pay attention to or notice, another meaning being to recognise or greet someone. Both senses are usually found in the negative, as in "She didna goam (did not notice) the car until it hit her." or "He didna goam his auld freen." (He didn't recognize his old friend.)

Goam, which was fairly common in some northern English dialects, has come down from Middle English *gome*, meaning understanding or discernment, and has connections with Old Norse *gaumr*, meaning heed or attention.

From *goam* is derived the adjective *goamless*. Yes, you have guessed right. *Goamless* means stupid or foolish. Still, you can never have too many words relating to stupidity, since there is such a lot of it about.

Favourite Scots Words

The English beat us to it as far as *goamless* is concerned. It appeared in northern English dialects before it came to Scots and is a forerunner of English *gormless*, meaning lacking intelligence, commonsense or initiative.

GREET

In English the verb *greet* means to say hello to someone, but the same verb has a completely different meaning in Scots, although the verbs probably have a common ancestor in Old English *gretan*. In Scots *greet* means to weep.

There are differences in grammar as well as meaning between the two verbs. The past tense of English *greet* is *greeted*, as in "He greeted them with a wave of the hand." The past tense of Scots *greet* can be either *gret* or *grat*.

Scots *greet* can also be a noun meaning a bout of weeping. So, when everything gets too much for you, you can sit down and have a right good *greet*, at least if you are a woman or child. I suspect macho man is still expected to have a stiff upper lip, at least in public.

Greet has given rise to such expressions as *greetin match*. A *greetin match* involves one or several of a group of children crying after an unfortunate incident of some kind. Like the English expression *it will end in tears*, this phrase is used prophetically by parents who can see the potential danger or mishap in some form of play. Children, of course, ignore such warnings.

Then there is *greetin face*. This can describe someone who looks permanently miserable, as though on the verge of tears. But it can also be used to describe someone who is never satisfied and who is always grumbling or moaning.

This is because *greet* has a secondary meaning. It started off meaning to shed tears, but it later also came to mean to complain or grumble. From this sense comes *greetin Teenie*, someone of either sex who always finds something to complain about. Like *greetin face*, it can also refer to someone with a permanently miserable expression.

What a pity that all *greet's* Scots connections are connected with misery or dissatisfaction when the English ones are so welcoming!

GUDDLE

A friend of mine once remarked that he often used Scots when talking to himself or thinking, but would translate this into Standard English when he was talking to someone else. This is true of quite a few of us.

I found myself doing it just the other day. I was trying to find something amid the piles of books and papers in the room where I work. The place, as I said to myself, was in a right *guddle*. However, I rephrased this as a bit of a muddle when talking on the phone to a friend from southern England. Undeniably, it lost something in translation.

Nowadays, a *guddle* usually refers to a state of confusion, disorder or untidiness. A person, a place or something such as a pile of paperwork can be *in a guddle*. If you *make a guddle of* something, you do it very badly and make a mess of it. There is a verb equivalent and to *guddle* is to work in a careless, untidy, messy way. To *guddle about* can be to mess about in an aimless way.

Guddle was originally associated with mess involving water. For example, children might be found *guddling about* in muddy puddles or a human restaurant dishwasher might spend ages *guddling about* in greasy, dirty water. In origin the word is thought to imitate the sound made by the action of guddling in water.

Guddle in its earliest sense is associated with fish as well as water. To *guddle* in this meaning is to try to catch fish using the hands only. This is done by groping under the hidden places in a stream or river where fish might be lurking. When the fish is located the fisher tickles the fish on its underbelly and pulls it out of the water.

Apparently this is an extremely difficult thing to do, though as a child I saw it done both successfully and effortlessly. A very old man who lived nearby was a real expert at *guddling* trout. It is, of course, an illegal pursuit, being a form of poaching. Fortunately, no-one ever shopped him and he is now well beyond the reach of the long arm of mortal law.

GUISING

Over the decades we have got used to the gross commercialization of Christmas, but the fact that the same fate has befallen Hallowe'en has taken many of us by surprise. Until comparatively recently, it was, in the UK at least, a comparatively low-key, homespun affair. The event was largely confined to Scotland and the highlight of the evening was children going *guising*.

Guising, pronounced like *disguising* with the first syllable of this omitted, involves dressing up as something or someone considered appropriate to Hallowe'en. This used to entail raiding the attic or the parental wardrobe for suitable material and adding a goodly dollop of imagination and improvisation.

Now it often entails visiting a shop and choosing something from its range of traditional Hallowe'en costumes, such ghosts, devils and witches, together with the witches' paraphernalia of black cats, broomsticks and cauldrons, and even fairies.If the witch is too ugly and the ghost too plain, there is always a cute cat costume or a pretty fairy outfit in black with a bit of sparkle.

When everyone is duly dressed up, off go the *guisers* (as they are called) to call on the people in nearby streets. When the neighbours open the door the children perform some sort of vaguely creative act, such as singing a song, reciting a poem or dancing a dance, and the neighbours hand over some kind of suitable treat, such as apples, nuts or sweets.

At least this is the theory and this was the former practice. Nowadays, if children go *guising* at all, and the tradition is much in decline, they often just shuffle about in their Hallowe'en costumes and either giggle uncontrollably or mumble something unintelligible. Because of worries about attack or abduction, the children are not infrequently accompanied by parents who want the whole thing to be over as soon as possible so that they can get back to the comfort of their own homes and a large G&T or glass of red wine. Meanwhile, the person who is at the receiving end of the so-called *guising* often just hands over a coin or coins, having had either no time or no inclination to stop and buy apples, nuts or sweets. This is very acceptable to the *guisers* as they are tired of eating apples as one of their five-a-day, they could well have a nut allergy and they are not allowed to eat sweets for fear of developing tooth cavities.

An increasing number of people in the houses selected by modern-day *guisers* appear to be not at home. Often they have simply decided not to answer the door. Some of them may have been put off the whole idea of Hallowe'en by the introduction of the seemingly sinister American "trick or treat". *Guisers* were bad enough, but they absolutely refuse to be threatened in their home. The door stays shut and the guisers go home dejected and moneyless, vowing not to bother next year — and another custom bites the dust.

Because Hallowe'en (31 October) and the fifth of November (the date of the festival associated with Guy Fawkes) are chronologically very close together, it is wrongly assumed by some non-Scots that the guy burned on the bonfire is somehow connected with the word *guising*, and that people asking for a penny for the guy are, in fact, *guising*. Not so.

The words *guising* and *guiser* come from the verb *guise*, meaning to disguise or dress up. This is related to the noun *guise* which meant a way of doing something, a fashion of dress, or a habit or custom before coming to mean masquerading or merry-making. This is related to the French word *guise*, a way or manner, and to the French verb *se deguiser*, to disguise yourself.

Historically, *guisers* were adults, often men who wore false faces and dressed up, sometimes in women's clothes. The Church disapproved of this and put a stop to it—spoilsports!

- H -

HAPPIT

When the Scottish winter comes it is time to make sure that we are *weel happit up*. Should you be unfamiliar with this phrase, it is the Scots equivalent of English *well wrapped up*, but more so.

Whenever I think of cold, snowy winter days, this expression comes back to me because I spent my early childhood winter days in a *weel happit up* state. It was basically the layered look, but long before this fashionable expression was coined and it certainly lacked the elegance that it suggests.

The basis of the *weel happit up* look was a vest or **semmit** or even, for girls, a liberty bodice. You will have to be pretty old to have worn one of these, because they ceased to be popular around the 1950s. A liberty bodice was a close-fitting sleeveless undergarment for the upper body made of thick soft cotton. It took its name from the fact that it was considerably less restrictive than its predecessor, the corset, but it was far from glamorous.

Over the vest, semmit or liberty bodice went several sweaters, usually wool and often scratchy, followed by jacket and coat. Then the accessories were piled on, scarf, hat and gloves, the gloves often being replaced on female hands by mittens, called **pawkies** in Scots.

And there you have it – the *weel happit up* look.

It was a look intended to keep you warm and cosy on freezing days, but it went further. It often made the wearer too hot and consequently sweaty, especially if he or she was hurrying to catch the school bus.

The word *happit* comes from the verb to *hap*, meaning to cover, often with the purpose of sheltering or concealing something. This has been in use in Scots since the 14th century and is derived from Middle English.

The verb *hap* can be used with reference to a person, as when "you hap an invalid up in a blanket" or "hap a child up in bed". It can also be used with reference to covering something such as potatoes or plants with earth or straw to protect them from the cold and wet.

Other uses include covering a corpse with earth in the grave and making up a fire so that it will continue to burn slowly for a while. Figuratively, it can be used of mist covering the tops of mountains or people *happing something away* that they might have need of later. *Hap* can also be a noun meaning a covering of some kind which provides protection against the weather. More specifically, it is used to refer to a shawl, plaid or outer garment, or to a blanket or quilt.

The *weel happit up* look is not nearly as common among children as it once was. Well, many of them don't really need to be wrapped in several layers nowadays, do they? After all, they only have to take a few steps from their front door to the vehicle that will whisk them away on the school run and fetch them back again. They see little of the great outdoors.

The real reason, however, that the *weel happit up* look is not popular among the young is that it is just not cool. Well, by very definition, you wouldn't expect it to be cool in terms of temperature – but it is not cool in terms of image, and image is everything these days. Many young people would not be seen dead in the *weel happit up* look, preferring to wear skimpy T-shirts and show off bare midriffs even in the coldest of winter days.

It is a wonder that more of them do not suffer from hypothermia. At least the *weel happit up* look prevents that.

HASH

I met an old friend the other day, but she had no time to stop and chat because she was running to catch a train which was scheduled to leave any minute. She was red of face, short of breath and in a state of advanced agitation. In other words she was *hashing* along.

The Scots verb to *hash* in this context means to move along in a very hurried, flustered way. Sometimes a person *hashes* along because of a lack of organization on their part. They are always in a state of excessive haste because they are chronically unpunctual or in a permanent muddle.

Sometimes, however, people *hash* along because they are the victims of what is now known as multi-tasking. They have to rush around frantically just to stay ahead of the game. This is probably why women are generally more given to *hashing* than the male of the species.

Haste is often not a good idea. Not only does it often make for less speed, but it also often makes for a botched job. It is not surprising, then, that the verb *hash* can also mean to do something in a hurried and clumsy or inexpert way. Careful craftsmen will take their time and achieve a perfect piece of work. Those who *hash* at a task will end up, at best, with something distinctly amateurish and below standard. The verb *hash* has several other meanings in Scots. One of these is to overwork or harass people so that they become fatigued or exhausted — sounds like the victims of multi-tasking again. Another meaning is to spoil, damage or destroy something — sometimes the result of those who *hash* at a task.

In origin, the verb *hash* is connected with the French verb *hacher* meaning to cut into small pieces. It is, therefore, quite logical that the earlier meanings of *hash* relate to cutting, as in to slash or hack, or to cut up into small pieces, as meat.

This may ring a few bells among English speakers and rightly so. In Scots, the noun *hash*, like the verb, has several meanings. In English it means a hot dish made up of cooked meat and potatoes cut into small pieces, as in *corned beef hash*.

The Scots noun *hash* can be used as a term of insult aimed at someone whom you consider to be stupid, clumsy, impertinent or generally undesirable. It commonly refers to a mess, muddle or state of chaos or to work done in a hurried, slapdash way.

The nearest English gets to any of the Scots meanings of the noun *hash* occurs in idiomatic phrases. One of these is *make a hash of* something, meaning to make a complete mess of it. The other is *settle someone's hash* meaning to subdue someone or prevent them from causing trouble.

While thinking about writing this piece I came across a Scots phrase that I find particularly appealing. *Hash and fash at* means to keep harping on about something or to make a great fuss about something. I think I will start using it.

HEID

Scots and English are linguistically related, both being descended from Anglo-Saxon. It is no wonder, then, that some words in one language are similar in form to words in the other. Thus, English has *head* and Scots has *heid*, pronounced to rhyme with "seed".

Like head in English, *heid* means the part of the body that houses the brain, the highest part of something or someone who is in charge of something. For example, the head of a school in English is a *heid* in Scots. However, in Scots this educational *heid* was, and is, often informally referred to as *the heidie*. English has not followed suit in this respect. There is no *headie*.

Favourite Scots Words

It is not really surprising that English does not have an equivalent of *heidie*. Words ending in "–ie" which indicate a diminutive form or an affectionate or familiar use, such as *postie* (a postman) or *beastie* (a small animal or insect), are much commoner in Scots than in English.

Some confusion once existed in parts of Scotland where *heid* or *heidie* could refer to the person at the top of the class as well as to the head teacher. Presumably, it was quite easy to tell them apart if you saw them together.

In Scots someone who is at the top level of an organization is often referred to as a *heid yin* (literally translated as a "head one"). If the person is even more important than such a position implies the term *high heid yin* is used. The term does not usually convey any sense of admiration since such people are not usually greeted with approval by the lower ranks. However, it can be used neutrally as well as disapprovingly.

Not so *heid bummer* which is bristling with disapproval or even contempt. A *heid bummer* is a person in charge, such as a senior manager or chief executive, a kind of Scots head honcho. It should not be confused with *heid-banger* which means a very stupid person or a wild, crazy person. This has an English equivalent--*head-banger*, but, somehow, this does not sound quite as insulting as the Scots version.

Heid, like head, can act as a verb. The verb originally meant to behead someone, although this meaning, like the practice, is now archaic. It can also mean to lead or be the head of, or to reach the summit of a hill or mountain. However, the verb *heid* is now mostly associated with one of our main national obsessions, football. For those whose obsessions do not include football, *heid* means to hit the ball with your head. This practice is known as *heidie*, and it has given rise to the expression *heid-the-baw* (=ball).

Here I become slightly puzzled. Some reference books indicate that *heid-the-baw* is used as a kind of nickname which can be used affectionately or to indicate that the person so-called is stupid. I have always heard it used, with no suggestion of affection, of someone who is considered to be extremely arrogant. What does it mean to you?

HEISE

Many Scots of a certain age will have memories of a Scots word used in their childhood and never encountered since. Trying to locate the word later in life can be tricky. Some words were local to some areas of the country and not to others. Thus even a contemporary fellow words enthusiast might not be aware of your particular word, if you come from different parts of Scotland.

Searching in reference books for a Scots word is a more formidable task than searching for an English word. The spread of printing in England set off a process that led to the standardization of spelling in English, but this did not happen in Scots. The result is that a great many Scots words have several possible spelling variants and this can greatly impede a word search.

The word I set out to chase up had certainly plenty of such variants. It appears that it could be spelt *heeze, heise,hese, hease, hyse, hize*, to name only some of the variants. I had only ever come across the word in speech and so I could only guess at a likely spelling on the basis of the pronunciation. It was pronounced to rhyme with *rise* and so I presumed it was spelt *heise* or *hize*, the former because the word sounded Germanic.

My thoughts on its roots proved accurate, because this word of so many variants comes from a Low German word *hissen* and has connections with Dutch *hijschen*. These words mean to raise or lift and are also related to the English word *hoist*.

Here I hit another problem. As the origin would suggest, the core meaning of Scots *heeze* is to lift, raise or hoist, also being used figuratively. To *heeze up your heart* is to raise your spirits or to cheer up.

All this is very interesting, but this was not the meaning of my youth. The word I was looking for meant to hurry, as in "They were late and were heisin up the road to catch the school bus."

Finally, I found this meaning – to travel fast, hasten, hurry – but it was far down quite a long list of meanings. These include to hurry or whisk someone away, to dance in a particularly lively way, or to enjoy yourself by making merry. Other meanings are to increase, as rents or prices, or to swarm or teem with, *heezin wi* being a synonym for Scots **hoachin wi**.

I still have not personaly found anyone who is familiar with the *heise/hize* spelling or the hurrying meaning. It was apparently more common in Perthshire and Kinross and so, if you hail from there, you might be familiar with it.

Back to *heeze* and *hoist*. Apparently there was a game called *heezie-hozie*, or *eezie-ozie*, in which two players stand back to back with arms interlinked.

They then stoop down alternately, raising the other from the ground as they stoop. Don't try this at home or someone might have to *heise* you to Accident and Emergency, especially if your partner in the game is considerably more substantial than you.

HEN

The Scots are traditionally known for their dourness and certainly not for their demonstrativeness. Not surprisingly, then, the Scots language is sparse in terms of endearment.

If you are seeking a Scots word of endearment for your loved one you could try *jo*. This can be applied to both sexes and has the advantage of being easy to find rhymes for if your thoughts turn to verse-writing. *Jo* has the alternative spelling *joe* and is, in origin, associated with the English word *joy*.

Jo was good enough for Robert Burns as in his poem "*John Anderson, my jo*", and so it is certainly good enough for amateur valentine writers. *Jo* is now used mostly in literary contexts, rather than in everyday communication. Still, your do-it-yourself valentine may be a work of literary art.

Perhaps the most famous Scots everyday endearment is *hen*. In Scots the word *hen* can be used as the name of a fowl in much the same way as it is in English, and it can be used instead of the English word *chicken*. Thus, the English chicken soup was often known *as hen-broth* or *hen-bree* and the English *chicken-hearted* translates into Scots as *hen-herted*.

A *hen-wife* was a woman employed to tend hens and other poultry. Interestingly, the term *hen-wife*, when applied to a man, is a man who is rather womanish and over-concerned with matters thought more appropriate to females.

As an endearment, *hen* is applied to members of the female of the species by members of either gender and is now more common in the west of the country than in the east. Like many so-called endearments, such as the English *love* and *dear*, *hen* is not just used to a female that the speaker is fond of.

True, it is often used to wives, girlfriends, daughters, other female members of the family or female friends. However, *hen* has become just a familiar form of address which can be directed at any female, whether she

Favourite Scots Words

is your best friend, a nodding acquaintance or a total stranger. You will find it regularly used by people in shops, bus drivers, taxi drivers and so on to their customers.

Hen, in common with *love, dear,* etc, is not always uttered in friendly tones when used as a form of address. Mostly, it is used unthinkingly in neutral tones, part of the bored and boring automatic exchanges of mundane, everyday life, but it can be used with irony or even hostility. A woman is likely to be greeted with a hostile "Thanks, hen." if she has unwittingly or intentionally upset someone. Her failure to give a big enough tip to a taxi driver (a serious offence) may elicit such a response.

Many woman resent being called hen. You cannot really blame them. It is hardly complimentary to be referred to as a farmyard fowl.

HOACHIN

Hoachin is not a pretty word and it is often intended to be not at all complimentary, although it is occasionally used simply as a neutral observation. It means extremely busy or overcrowded. Those who use the word are often complaining about the huge crowds, such as tourists or Christmas shoppers, who are thronging the streets and roads and preventing people from getting on with their ordinary lives.

The first syllable of *hoachin*, which can be spelt *hoatchin*, is pronounced to rhyme with *coach*. The original form of the word is *hotchin*. This can be pronounced as *hoachin* or the first syllable can be pronounced to rhyme with *cot*. All forms still exist.

Hoachin and its alternatives can also mean infested with or swarming with something unpleasant. You will find it used frequently of that ferocious enemy of tourists to Scotland, midges. Places that are *hoachin wi midges* are soon cleared of tourists. The word can also be used of vermin of various kinds and so dogs can be *hoachin wi fleas* or heads *hoachin wi lice*. I feel itchy at the very thought.

Before it became associated with teeming or infested, *hotchin* meant fidgety, either from impatience or discomfort, or seething with eagerness to do something. It is derived from the verb *hotch* in its sense of to fidget or be restless. The original meaning of the verb *hotch* is to move jerkily up and down, to bob up and down. It can also be used to mean to laugh extremely heartily or to move along when you are sitting down in order to make room for someone else. *Hotch* can also be a noun with meanings corresponding to those of the verb, for example jerk, jolt, bounce. However, it can also be used of an untidy mess or state of disorder and it stays with its messy associations when it is applied to a big, fat, ungainly, sluttish woman. Not a pretty sight!

Like many Scots words, the use of *hoachin*, or either of its alternatives, does not stop at the border. It has found its way into at least northern England. As to origin, the verb may have connections with Dutch *hotsen*, to jog or jolt and German *hotzen*, to move up and down.

HOGMANAY

Like Christmas, *Hogmanay*, Scots for New Year's Eve, is associated with eating and drinking, although not usually now in that order of importance. Formerly, though, *Hogmanay* was more associated with eating, particularly if you were a child. It was the custom for children to go round the houses asking for a gift, usually a cake or something sweet, giving the festival the name of *Cake Day*.

Incidentally, the giving of gifts on *Hogmanay* is thought by many people to have a bearing on the origin of the word *Hogmanay*, although the etymology is uncertain. The most widely accepted suggested origin is that *Hogmanay* is based on the French word *aguillanneuf*, meaning first a gift given at New Year and then the festival of New Year itself. The clue is in the second part of the French word which reads *l'an neuf*, French for New Year.

Nowadays, *Hogmanay* is still associated with the giving of gifts and it is thought to bring ill-luck to a household if a visitor crosses the threshold in the early hours of New Year without some form of gift. This is particularly true if the empty-handed visitor is the first foot, *first fit* in Scots, the first person to cross a threshold after midnight has struck.

Sometimes New Year gifts still take the form of sweet things such as shortbread or the immensely calorific black bun, a kind of cake consisting of a pastry case surrounding an extremely rich fruitcake mixture. Sometimes the gift will be a piece of coal, traditionally given to ensure a steady source of warmth throughout the year, although this could be a vain hope in these days of soaring fuel costs.

Mostly nowadays, though, visitors at New Year will be clutching a bottle of whisky. Unless they are exceptionally generous or exceptionally drunk, the bottle of whisky is not actually a gift. The gift for the host is just a glass poured from the bottle which is hastily put back in the visitor's pocket.

HOWK

The Scots verb *howk*, in which the "ow" sound rhymes with "wow", is a later form of Scots *holk*, which has connections with Middle English *holk* and an old German verb *holken* meaning to dig. *Howk's* original meaning was also to dig, as in to dig a trench, and then it went on to mean also to uproot or extricate. As is the case with *howking out* dandelions, there is an underlying sense that the process of *howking* is an arduous task.

We tend to associate *howking* with tatties, or potatoes to the less well-informed. I can speak with some experience of *tattie-howkin* as I am of that generation for whom the tattie holidays in October, if you lived in rural parts and needed the money, often involved such a back-breaking task. Nowadays, the October school holiday is sometimes still known in some quarters as the "tattie holidays", but the humble tatties are no longer involved. The tattie fields have long ago been replaced as a holiday venue by Spanish beaches or somewhere more exotic.

At least in my day, *tattie-howkin* did not involve actual digging. This process was carried out by a tractor-pulled mechanical digger. Picking the tatties, however, was still arduous and it was murder on the back. No wonder the expression *howk-backit*, having a bent back, arose. If you spent long enough lifting potatoes you could very easily end up with one.

My other personal experience of *howkin* involved *neeps* (turnips or swedes), not tatties. When my children were young "trick or treat" had yet to invade our shores and there was no such thing as a pumpkin lantern at Halloween. Light at Halloween had to be provided by a candle in a *howked-out neep*. *Howkin* out the middle of a turnip was very hard on the hands and it was certainly not a job for the nail-proud. *Howk* was also used to mean excavate coal from a mine. No, I have not actually tried that, but I had relatives who did. If you have a persistently painful tooth and do not want to go near a dentist, you can *howk* it out by a tying one end of a piece of string to the tooth and the other to a door knob before slamming the door. End of tooth and toothache, hopefully. Staying with body parts, you can also *howk* your nose, but do not do so in polite society. Seeing someone picking their nose is not a pretty sight.

The verb *howk* can be used figuratively to mean to unearth something or to bring something to light, in the same way that *dig* can. So you can *howk* out an old forgotten book from the attic to lend to a friend. *Howk* can also be part of an investigative process. It can either be used to refer to legitimate research or to unwanted, interfering nose-poking.

As you will have seen, *howk* mostly involves a great deal of work. However, another sense of the word crept in. *Howk* can also mean to stand around idly or loaf about. That sounds altogether a much more pleasant prospect than *howkin* either tatties or dandelions.

HUMPH

The word *humph* in English dictionaries is usually defined as an interjection indicating annoyance, dissatisfaction, disgust or doubt. I am not sure that I have actually ever heard anyone pronouncing the word as it is spelt. It usually comes out as a kind of grunt or growl.

In Scots the word *humph* might easily come accompanied by a series of grunts because it means to carry around something heavy. Before the days when suitcases came equipped with handy little wheels, *humphin* your luggage around airports or railway stations was an all too common part of the holiday experience.

But we still *humph* overflowing bags of shopping from supermarket to car and car to house unless we are going by bus or on foot, in which case the *humphin* process is likely to be accompanied by even more grunts. Also fond parents are obliged to *humph* around their small children when they claim to be too tired to walk. It is strange how the children do not seem to be quite so small after half a mile or so of this activity.

The verb *humph* can also mean to move around with great difficulty because you are carrying a heavy or unwieldy load. Thus you might see pupils from the local school *humphin* up the road clutching the many bags that some of them seem to need these day, while somehow still leaving a hand free to clutch their mobile phones.

In origin, *humph* is a Scots form of English *hump*, as in a curvature of the back. In Scots, English *hunched* becomes *humphed* and *hunch-backed* becomes *humph-backed* or *humphie-backit*. *Humph* has given rise to a number of interesting phrases.

The phrase to *come up yir humph* means to occur to you, to come into your

Favourite Scots Words

head, as in " He might meet us off the train if it comes up his humph." However, the phrase *gae up yir humph* means to be beyond your powers of understanding or to be a mystery to you, as in "Why she left sae (=so) suddenly gaes (=goes) up ma humph." If you *set up yir humph* you get very angry and hostile, as in "He really sets up ma humph when he starts bragging."

If you are tired of someone's company and want to be rid of them you can use the fairly modern informal expression *awa* (=away) *an run up ma humph*. This is certainly more picturesque than the English interjection *get lost*. Even more picturesque is *awa and cuddle my humph*. No thanks.

There is another Scots word *humph*, with the alternative spelling *humf*, which is unrelated to the one just described. This one may be derived from the English interjection that I started off with. It means to have or acquire an offensive smell or taste, as of something decaying or rotting lying forgotten at the back of your fridge.

If something is giving off a horrible smell it can be described as *humphed* or *humphy*. They are more or less synonyms for **mingin**, meaning stinking, but they have not acquired its popular figurative uses. Probably for this reason, *humphy* has not achieved the export success that **mingin** has. It has stayed at home.

HUNKER

It is a sure sign of getting old when your joints begin to play up. They start to creak, stiffen up and cause sudden stabs of pain, making actions like *hunkering* very difficult. Even trickier is the process of getting up after *hunkering*.

The verb to *hunker*, more commonly to *hunker doon* (=down), is a Scots term meaning to crouch down, sitting on your haunches. The English equivalent is *squat*, which is rather an ugly word and is not infrequently associated with excretion.

The verb *hunker*, thought to be derived from a Germanic word which is also likely to be the source of Old Norse *huka* and German *hocken*, meaning to crouch or to squat, can also mean to huddle, as in *hunkerin roon* a small fire in an attempt to get warm. Figuratively, it is used to mean to submit to someone or something, as in having to *hunker doon* to the demands of a tyrant. You can also be obliged to *hunker doon* to circumstances, meaning that you resign yourself to the difficulties of whatever situation you find yourself in. You have no choice.

Hunker is one of these expressions which was exported from Scotland to America, without stopping off in England. There it began to be followed by *down* rather than *doon*. While in America *hunker down* spread its wings and developed other meanings. When you are sitting on your haunches you are less visible than you are when you are standing up, at least from some angles. So it is quite logical that *hunker down* came to mean to hide or hide out, whatever physical position you adopted in the process.

This was just a step away from its meaning of to settle in a relatively comfortable or safe place for an extended period of time while things improve. This sense can be used literally or figuratively, as in to *hunker down* in the cabin over the long winter or to *hunker down* and spend as little money as possible during a recession.

Other meanings developed. *Hunker down* came to mean to refuse absolutely to change your opinion, attitude, way of behaving etc, to stick your principles, so to speak. Next came to make preparations for the undertaking of a difficult task, to buckle down to something. If students find exams looming they would do well to *hunker down* and get some studying done.

What happened to *hunker down* next? The American meanings were exported to the UK, this time to English. *Hunker doon* had become a transatlantic success story.

Hunker as a noun, although usually in the plural form *hunkers*, is also commonly found in Scots. The *hunkers* are the haunches or the backs of the thighs, the part of the body that you balance yourself on when you *hunker doon*. Sitting on your *hunkers* is by no means a comfortable position. If you are *on your hunkers* figuratively you are in trouble, often serious trouble and often trouble of a financial nature. It is like being on your last legs or your beam ends.

HURDIES

The Scots poet Robert Burns has gained world-wide fame and many countries join with Scotland in celebrating his birthday on January 26. In honour of this many Burns suppers take place across the globe.

These can be quite formal affairs and one of the traditions associated with

Favourite Scots Words

these is the addressing of the haggis. In other words someone stands before the haggis and recites the words of the *Address to the Haggis*, written by Robert Burns. Many people who are called upon to do so feel distinctly nervous.

The reason for their disquiet is quite often linguistic in nature. The people in question may be Scots, but their knowledge of the language may be hazy in the extreme. Yet they somehow have to get their tongues round words which are unfamiliar to them and, worse, memorise them.

One of the early problem words which they encounter is *hurdies*, as in:

> *The groaning trencher there ye fill,*
> *Yir hurdies like a distant hill,*
> *Yir pin wad help to mend a mill*
> *In time o' need,*
> *While thro' your pores the dews distil*
> *Like amber bead.*

What on earth does *hurdies* mean?

Technically a haggis does not really have *hurdies*, but what's a bit of poetic licence between friends? *Hurdies* are reserved for humans and animals. The word means the buttocks, hips or haunches. Burns used it again in Tam o Shanter, this time of a human, the poet himself:

> *Thir breeks o' mine, my only pair,*
> *That aince were plush, o' guid blue hair,*
> *I wud hae gien them off my hurdies,*
> *For ae blink o' the bonie burdies!*

For those of you who are not up to speed with your Tam o Shanter this means that the poet would have given the trousers off his buttocks for the sight of some beautiful young women. In fact, he probably frequently did.

Hurdies is pronounced as it is spelt, but do not forget the "r". It has been around the Scots language since the sixteenth century and its origins are lost in the mists of time.

The word has faded a bit from popular use, perhaps because it sounds a bit too solid for an age when hips are not really acceptable till they are need in of replacement. I cannot really see the question "Do my hurdies look big in this?" catching on.

The word *hurdies* supplies us with a phrase to describe a situation which is all too common in these difficult times. The expression is *ower* (=over) *the hurdies* meaning in financial difficulties, deep in debt. Well, I suppose it is not quite as bad as being up to the ears, eyes or neck in debt.

HURL

Confusion can occur when a Scots word and an English word have the same form and pronunciation, but different meanings. Take, for example, the verb *hurl*. Scots cyclists might say that they had to *hurl* their bikes up the steepest part of an incline, leaving English listeners to wonder why the cyclists were throwing their treasured bikes violently up the hill. It seems like a waste of a good bike.

Scots might also say "We've put the baby in the pram and her grandfather's hurling it up and down the garden path." The cognoscenti will know that the said grandfather is pushing the pram up and down the garden path, probably with a view to getting the baby to go to sleep. Some unsuspecting English person might think, however unlikely, that the grandfather is throwing the pram with great force up and down the garden path-- and hurriedly get in touch with social services.

If you have been paying attention you will by now have deduced that, while in English the verb *hurl* means to throw something with great force, in Scots it means to push or pull something along on wheels or to transport someone or something in a wheeled vehicle. The English and Scots words are related and may both have their origins in the fact that the words imitate the sound made by the action of the verb.

Hurl in Scots can mean to move along on wheels or to be transported in a wheeled vehicle. Thus, you might find yourself *hurlin* along the motorway to your destination, hopefully not at an excessive speed. Another meaning is to fall from a great height, as masonry falling from a high building in hurricane-style winds.

In Scots hurl can also be a noun with meanings corresponding to those of the verb. The last-mentioned verb has a corresponding noun meaning a violent rush downwards or forwards, as in a *hurl* of heavy snow or a *hurl* of masonry falling from a dilapidated building.

Much more commonly, though, the noun *hurl* means a ride or drive in a wheeled vehicle. Thus, you might hear children demanding a *hurl* in a relative's brand new car. Alternatively, you might hear them requesting a

Favourite Scots Words

hurl in a shopping trolley to save them the effort of trudging around the store. They then get a better view of what is on offer on the shelves which can make their pester power more effective.

You can request a *hurl* to somewhere instead of asking for a lift. If you are in a *hurl* you find yourself in a confused mass and surrounded by noise, as in a crowded shop at Christmas time.

A *hurl-barrow* or a *hurlie-barrow* is a wheelbarrow, while a *hurl-cairt* is a cart as used by farmers etc. A *hurlie-cairt* can be an ordinary cart, although it often refers to a child's home-made cart of the kind made by fixing makeshift wheels on an orange box. Staying with wheelbarrows, to *speir* (=ask) *the guts oot o a hurl-barrie* (=barrow) is to be over-inquisitive and ask too many questions.

A *hurl-bed* or *hurlie-bed* is a low bed with wheels or casters that can be pushed under another bed. This is sometimes known in English as a *truckle bed* and in American English as a *trundle bed*. Whatever you call them, they used to be very commonly used when families were larger and space was at a premium.

A *hurley-gush* has several meanings. Originally, it was used to refer to a noisy surge of water or a body of water in spate. It then went on to be used figuratively to refer to someone who talks too much and then to be used as a synonym for garrulousness or verbosity. This is known informally in English as *verbal diarrhoea*.

In fact, *hurley-gush* can be used to refer to the original, non-verbal diarrhoea also. *Hurley-gush* is a much more pleasant word than diarrhoea for the over-swift voiding of bodily waste.

- J -

JAG

There are considerably fewer deaths among young children than there were some decades ago. This improvement, to a significant extent, can be put down to the use of vaccinations which have prevented children from contracting many infectious diseases. However, many of us prefer not to use the word vaccination or even injection. We opt for something more informal, perhaps to make the experience sound less medical and so less scary.

In English the informal word often used is *jab*, the same word that is used to describe a short sharp punching movement of the kind used in boxing. As is often the case, the Scots word for vaccination or injection is nearer the mark, so to speak.

The word is *jag* and it somehow describes the sharp and sometimes painful experience of vaccination more aptly. A *jab* may sound painful but it does not capture the piercing effect of the needle sinking into flesh. Somehow *jag* does.

The word *jag* in Scots has been around a lot longer than the process of vaccination. It came into being in the very early sixteenth century meaning to pierce, later coming to mean also to feel pain resulting from being pierced with something sharp. In origin, it is probably descriptive of the action involved in piercing.

The noun equivalent was originally used to refer to a thorn or prickle, as of Scotland's emblematic thistle, or anything else which pierces or stings. It is also used to describe the action of piercing or stabbing with a sharp instrument like the needle on a hypodermic syringe.

From *jag* comes the adjective *jaggy* or *jaggie* meaning prickly, piercing or sharp-pointed. It is used of obviously prickly things such as thistles and barbed wire is known as *jaggy wire*. However, nettles are also frequently referred to as *jaggy* because of the painful stings that they impart to bare limbs.

Jag is one of those Scots words that do not obviously reveal their origins. It does not sound Scots and many people may use it without realizing that it is Scots. In fact, the word *jag* does exist in English but with different

Favourite Scots Words

meanings. It can refer to a sharp projection like a piece of rock and from this comes *jagged*, meaning with rough, pointed, often sharp edges.

English *jag* can also refer to a short period of time spent over-indulging in a particular activity such as shopping or weeping. This sense often relates to a period of time spent downing excessive quantities of alcohol, as when binge-drinking.

In this alcoholic respect English *jag* has a connection with Scots *jag* which, apart from the meanings already given, can mean a shot of alcohol. Some adults with a needle phobia may feel the need of such a *jag* before going for a vaccination or injection.

JANITOR

British English adopts a great many slang and trendy terms from American English. Yet, as far as the everyday vocabularies are concerned, there are many differences between the two languages. We stick to our pavements and they stick to their sidewalks. We look under car bonnets and they look under hoods and so on.

There are some words in American English which appear in Scots, although not in English. One of these is **pinkie**. Another is *janitor* which translates into English as caretaker.

In Scotland, *janitors* are usually to be found in schools where they are mostly known as *jannies*. The duties of a *jannie* are many and varied and include being in charge of the keys, attending to anything, such as the heating system, that needs fixed, and making sure that the school is clean.

Formerly, the *janitor* might also be made responsible for making sure that everyone who should be at school was actually there. He often acted as the attendance officer who rounded up those who were playing truant.

Earlier still, a *janitor* might be involved in the discipline of schoolchildren, in basic teaching and in more menial tasks around the school. In those days a *janitor* was frequently a poor person who paid for his own education by performing the afore-mentioned duties.

In America, the word *janitor* has wider applications. It is used of someone in charge of the maintenance in other public buildings as well as schools and colleges, and is also applied to a caretaker of an apartment building.

Nothing stays the same and this is as true of language as of anything else. I understand that in public high schools and colleges in parts of America the *janitor* is now often called the *custodian*. Hitherto, the term *custodian* was reserved for someone who looked after something particularly valuable, such as an art collection. Still, what could be more valuable than children?

I wondered whether a similar change had befallen *janitor* in Scotland and asked around. When I asked various children and teachers what they called a school *janitor*, most of them replied *jannie*, and a few said *janitor*. One very young relative said she called the school janitor "Mr Henderson". Quite right, too!

In these days when a spade is hardly ever known as a spade, and grandiose terms have taken over our lives, I thought it unlikely that *janitor* was still the official term. I duly rang the appropriate department in Edinburgh City Council and was told that the official term for a school janitor is *service support officer*. Whether this is confined to Edinburgh I know not. I rather doubt it. If it is, some other high-flown term will be in use elsewhere.

Janitor was originally used of a doorkeeper and it is derived from the Latin word for this, *ianitor*. The Latin word is associated with the Roman god Janus who was the god of gates, doors and also the god of beginnings and endings. His name gave rise to the month of January.

Janus had the advantage of having two faces, one at the front and one at the back, and so was able to look both ways. I am sure many custodians of children envy him this ability.

JOCO

Joco is a Scots word meaning happy, cheerful, or very pleased with yourself. It is a short, pert word that somehow manages to convey its meaning very well.

You might well feel *joco* if you have just enjoyed some kind of triumph. It is a bit like *cock-a-hoop*, but usually slightly more restrained. For example, the boss agreeing to give you an increase in salary would very likely make you feel *joco*, if astounded.

Finding a once-in-a-lifetime bargain in the January sales or watching your football team achieve an unexpected and decisive victory might also leave you feeling *joco*. Whatever makes you happy! *Joco* can also have the sense of unperturbed, relaxed or indifferent. Circumstances that might leave most of us nervous, agitated or even terrified might leave those with cooler heads quite *joco*, as in "That car missed him by inches, but he walked away, quite *joco*."

Joco is pronounced with the emphasis on the second syllable which rhymes with "low". It has several alternative spellings, including *jocko*, but, in this sense, it has nothing to do with the name *Jock*. Instead, it is a shortened form of the English word *jocose*. Unlike *joco*, *jocose* is rather a formal or literary word. It is often used to describe someone who is fond of joking and can also mean humorous or playful.

Jocose, and so *joco*, has its origins in Latin. It comes from the Latin word *jocosus* which is derived from Latin *jocus*, a joke. *Jocus* is also the source of the English word *jocular* meaning intended to be funny or fond of joking.

I said above that *joco* has nothing to do with the name Jock. On reflection, I should say that this is not completely true. In these days of innovative baby names *Joco* as a forename is a form of *Jock* which, in turn, is a Scots form of *John*. It is most common in America, but, no doubt, *Joco* will be coming soon to a baby near you.

JOUK

The origin of the Scots word *jouk*, pronounced to rhyme with "look", is a bit uncertain, but it is thought to be a variant of the Scots verb *dook*, as in to *dook* for apples at Halloween. This is the equivalent of the English verb to *duck*, derived from Old English *ducan*. *Jouk* is a short, swift word used to describe a short, swift action, usually one of an evasive nature.

The verb *jouk* can be used in various ways. Should you, for example, spot someone that you want to avoid—you may owe them money, not have the time to listen to their woes for half-an-hour, be unwilling to donate to their charity or just dislike them a great deal—you can *jouk* into the nearest shop or *jouk* up a handy side street.

Such evasive action is often undertaken to avoid someone in authority. School children who are kicking a ball around a park when they should be ensconced behind their desks would do well to *jouk* behind a shed or an exceptionally large tree should they catch sight of a teacher. Likewise, someone in possession of stolen goods would be wise to *jouk* somewhere out of sight should a police officer hove into view. Jouk can be used in the phrase *jouk the school*, to play truant. It can also be used before other nouns, often indicating someone or something that represents some kind of threat and so should be avoided. Thus, children who have just broken a window with their ball will try to *jouk* the irate house-owner who is after their blood. Someone who has committed a crime may be deemed fortunate to have *jouked* a jail sentence and got away with a fine or community service.

Jouk can also be used to mean to dodge a blow. You can either *jouk* nimbly out of the way of the blow or you can *jouk* your head and let the blow land somewhere where it will do less damage. This attempt to avoid a blow to the head gives rise to the proverb *It's ower late to jouk when the heid's aff.* This translates literally as "It's too late to dodge a blow to the head when the head is off." You cannot dispute the truth of that.

The verb *jouk* can also be used to mean to dart in and out. A nimble football player might be seen *jouking* his way in and out of the opposing team's defence. A seasoned and enthusiastic shopper might *jouk* in and out of crowds of Christmas shoppers to get to the front of the queue. (Me? I just give up and go home go home.) Also, a trout might *jouk* about in the water—merrily enjoying life until it is caught.

Jouk has given rise to another proverb to guide us on our way through life. This is *jouk an let the jaw gae by*. *Jaw* in this sense does not refer to a part of the face, but to a large wave or breaker. Literally this proverb means to duck to avoid an oncoming wave. Figuratively, it means if you are faced with an overpowering set of unfortunate circumstances, just submit to them. Do not try to fight them.

I am not sure that this call for passivity is good advice, particularly. The line of least resistance is the easy way out, but not necessarily the most effective.

Incidentally *jouk* may well have played a part in the formation of the expression *joukerie-pawkerie*. This means deceit, trickery or underhand dealings and it may well be the source of English *jiggery-pokery*. If *jouk* played a part in this then it teamed up with **pawkie** to do so. Look there for more information.

- K -

KALE

When browsing through the menus of some fairly upmarket restaurants recently I was surprised to see how many of these were offering dishes featuring *kale*. Of these *kale mash* was the most popular, but *kale* also appeared as a common accompanying vegetable—perhaps it is the new peas—and even as the main ingredient of a savoury tart.

Clearly *kale* is now regarded as posh nosh. This seems odd to me as I am sure that I regarded it as being mainly animal fodder when I was a child. You must remember that I am not young any more. Those of you who have not undergone the *kale* culinary experience may not even know what it is. *Kale* is, in fact, a kind of cabbage with dark green curly leaves. According to one dictionary, it is distinguishable from some other cabbages by having no heart—shades of the Tin Man in the Wizard of Oz.

Kale, better known in Scots as *kail* and the equivalent of English *cole*, derived from Old English, was once a staple of the Scots diet. After all, we were a poor country and it did not face much competition. So central to the Scots diet was *kail* that at one point in the nineteenth century it came to mean also a meal in itself, often the main meal of the day.

Kail also came to be used of soup, originally one made with *kail* leaves, but later extended to soup made from any vegetables or even meat. That is my main childhood memory of *kail*, a generic word for soup. If you wanted to specify the kind of soup you could always prefix the word *kail* with the main ingredient, as leek *kail*.

Kail also appeared in a dish known as *kail-kenny* or *kail-kennin* which consisted of potatoes and *kail* or cabbage mashed together. It is the equivalent of the Irish dish *colcannon*. Could it be the origin of the *kale mash* of restaurant fame?

The stalk of the *kail* plant is known either as a *kail-stock* or a *kail-runt*. This was the subject of an old Halloween tradition. A group of young people, sometimes blindfolded, were taken to a field after dark where they would pull kail- runts.

The shape of the runt they pulled was supposed to be an indication of the stature of their future spouse. Presumably everyone was hoping for a long and straight runt rather than a short and shrivelled one. Incidentally, a *kail-runt* can also be an insulting name for an old woman.

A *kailyard* was originally used to refer to a place where *kail* was grown, then coming to mean a kitchen garden. The expression is, however, better known for its literary connection. The *Kailyard* school of writing was coined to refer to a group of Scottish writers, such as J M Barrie, who wrote about rural domestic life in Scotland at the end of the nineteenth century. Unfortunately, it was rather too sentimental for many tastes, certainly modern tastes, and it is often used as a distinctly unflattering designation.

Kail features in a number of rather vivid sayings. Of these the most common is *cauld kail het again*, literally meaning cold soup or food reheated, and used to refer to something that you have heard over and over again until you are absolutely sick of it. The ramblings of some politicians are often a case in point.

Get yir kail het means literally to get your soup hot, but figuratively, it means to get a severe scolding. *Scaud yir lips in ither folk's kail*, means literally to scald your lips in other people's soup and figuratively to interfere or meddle in the affairs of others.

Idiomatically, *mak saut to yir kail* is something that is getting more and more difficult to do in these modern recessionary times. *Saut* is Scots for salt, but the expression means make a living.

KEEK

I was in a bus the other day when a toddler was attempting to get the rest of the passengers to join in her game. She was covering her eyes with her scarf, then removing it and shouting out "keek". Most of the passengers took part with enthusiasm, even those who obviously had no idea what *keek* means. Still, they got the essential message of the game which in Scotland is called *keek*, *keekboo* or *keekaboo* and in England *peekaboo*.

The game is derived from the Scots verb *keek* which means to take a quick look at something. The quick look often involves some degree of secrecy, inquisitiveness, or surreptitiousness. A nosey neighbour might *keek* through a chink in the curtains to see what their neighbour is up to. A would-be cheat might try and *keek* at someone else's answers during a school test. *Keek* can also be a noun with meanings corresponding to that of the verb. Thus, before venturing into a restaurant you might try and get a

Favourite Scots Words

quick *keek* at the menu so that you can make sure that there is something on it that you will like—and be able to afford. Fortunately, many restaurants now take the surreptitiousness out of *keeking* by displaying the menu in the window.

If you decide to *keek in on* someone you pay them a short visit, often unannounced. This visit is known, not surprisingly, as a *keek*. Remember that not everyone is enthused by such unscheduled *keeks*.

Keek, which is pronounced as it is spelt, appeared in Scots in the late fifteenth century. It is derived from Middle English *kiken* or *keken* and has connections with Dutch *kijken* to peep or look.

Keek has given rise to various compounds or phrases. *Keekin-glass* is a looking-glass or mirror, reminding us of those vain people who cannot pass anything shiny without having a quick *keek* to check on their reflection. A *keek-hole* is a *peep-hole*, a chink in something through which an inquisitive person can *keek* in order to satisfy their curiosity. Rather poetically *keek o' day* is dawn or sunrise and *keek o' noon* is midday.

A *keek-the-vennel* is a nickname given to a school attendance officer who was out to identify truants and bring retribution to them. A *vennel* is a lane or an alley. Presumably the attendance officer was always taking quick looks up such alleys with a view to glimpsing those who should have been safely behind their school desks. In similar vein a *keek-roon-corners* is a spy, *roon* meaning round.

The best-known derivative of *keek* nowadays is *keeker*. This originally referred to a person who *keeks* and was particularly used of a peeping Tom. It then went on to mean the eye, the organ that is *keeked* through. *Keeker* is also used to refer to a microscope, a *far-keeker* being a telescope.

However, these are violent times and the most appropriate meaning of *keeker* for such times is black eye, sometimes known as a *blue keeker*. Allegedly, such *keekers* are most commonly caused by walking into doors!

KEN

We are all more conscious of, and more critical of, other people's irritating habits than we are of our own. This includes speech habits. One of these is the use of linguistic fillers that do not add anything to what we want to say. You know the kind of thing.

Favourite Scots Words

One acquaintance begins practically every sentence with "Actually". Another routinely opens sentences with "basically". Yet another drives you mad by ending most sentences with "you know what I mean". In Scots such an add-on phrase is *ye ken*, meaning you know, as in "He's never been any good, ye ken." Or "This weather's gey depressing, ye ken."

The phrase *ye ken* is often shortened to ken. This is a very common Scots filler and in the case of some areas or some people the use of ken in this context can reach epidemic proportions. Examples include "He's at uni (university), ken." " I got laid off, ken." "They've got a new car, ken." or "We're, ken, struggling a bit." Often the person who is being addressed has no knowledge of what it is that they are supposed to know.

The verb ken can mean "know" with reference to facts, people or places. So you can say "He kens fine whit happened." "Naebody kens that man." or "They ken this city weel." The past tense of ken is kent, as in *We kent he wis ill*. The expression *I kent his faither* is a common Scottish expression used as a put-down for someone who has achieved outstanding success, especially given the circumstances. The implication is that if you knew their father then they cannot be up to much. We Scots do not like people to get above themselves. Upward mobility is out.

Kent can also be used as an adjective meaning known or familiar. You might say "The church was full of kent faces." or "I felt a bit lonely until I heard some kent voices." You can add an adverb to the kent for emphasis, as in "There were a few weel-kent faces in the court to support him."

Ken can function as a noun as well as a verb, meaning knowledge, acquaintance, comprehension or insight. It can also refer to the scope or limits of one's understanding, knowledge, or experience. This may very well call to mind the English phrase beyond my ken, as in "It is beyond my ken how he puts up with living there."

This Scots/English connection is quite understandable. *Ken* is derived from Middle English *kennen* and ultimately from Old English *cennan*, to make known, also being connected with Old Norse *kenna*. *Ken* is obsolete in English, apart from the *beyond my ken* meaning, but it is alive and thriving in Scots, although the verb *knaw,* Scots for know, also exists.

Kenna was once the common negative form of *ken*. Now it is usually *dinnae ken* or *dinna ken,* translated into English as *don't know*. In spoken Scots this often becomes *dinny ken* or *d'ken*.

73

- L -

LUG

Lug is not a pretty word and this is reflected in its meaning in English. The word means to carry or drag something heavy with a great deal of effort. It conjures up images of heavily laden people almost having their arms pulled out of their sockets by the weight of their luggage or shopping bags. You see them all the time at airports staggering from the car park towards the line of trolleys.

In Scots the meaning of *lug* is more neutral in terms of attractiveness. It can refer to something pretty or to something decidedly unattractive. That all depends on the person sporting them, for *lug* in Scots means an ear. *Lugs* come in all shapes and sizes, from the shell-like and discreet to the decidedly sticky-out and prominent.

At first *lug,* which is Scandinavian in origin and came into Scots in the fifteenth century, was applied only to the outer ear, to the part that protrudes from the sides of the head. Then it went on to be used of the inner workings that enable us to hear, as in *lug-drum* or *lug-ache.*

Because it is in the nature of ears to jut out they tend to be an easy target for those who want to inflict pain on the owner of the ears. A good tug or twist of the *lugs*, as well as a box, can be very painful. This used to be the kind of punishment that might be inflicted on small boys as a warning by, say, the local policeman, but this, of course, is no longer allowed.

Historically, *lugs* were involved in much more serious and much more formal forms of punishment. Those convicted of a crime might have had a nail put through their *lug* or they might even have it cut off. Ouch!

The word *lug* can refer to an animal's ear as well as to that of a human, but it can also be applied to parts of inanimate objects. *Lug* was first used of the flaps of a cap. It then went on to be used of the projecting parts of a receptacle used as handles. These are often found in pairs, as in a *quaich* (=a shallow bowl-shaped drinking vessel now much favoured as a christening present) and such receptacles are described as being *luggi*t. A *luggie* is a small wooden bowl with one *lug* or two that was often used for serving milk with porridge.

Historically, *lug* was used to refer to a concealed recess in a room from which a person could overhear a conversation with out being seen. Check out your rooms carefully if you have an old house! To some extent, the success of the eavesdropping would depend on the *lug-length*, the range of hearing, between the eavesdropper and those holding the conversation. Of course, you do not need such a recess to overhear other people's conversations. You *can lug-latch* or eavesdrop anywhere if you are careful.

As with many Scots words, *lug* appears in several colourful phrases, many of which have faded from use. Some *lug* phrases simply translate English ear phrases, as *up to the lugs in*, up to the ears in, while some are slightly different, as *lauch on the ither side o yir lug*, laugh on the other side of your face.

However many *lug* phrases are more unusual. If you *hae the wrang soo by the lug* you literally have the wrong pig by the *lug* and, figuratively, have come to the wrong conclusion. If you *get yir lug in yir luif* you literally get your ear in the palm of your hand and, figuratively, you get severely scolded.

The act of blowing in someone's ear usually has romantic overtones. This is not necessarily so as far as *blaw in the lug o* is concerned. This means to wheedle or cajole, whatever the nature of what the wheedler wants. Perhaps the most unusual *lug* phrase is the interjection *a pudding lug!* meaning nonsense. Somehow I cannot see this being revived into popular use.

Lug also makes an appearance in several proverbs. Good advice is *wide lugs and a short tongue are best*, meaning listen a good deal and say little. Finally, a warning to anyone who raises a glass. *Pint stoups* (=drinking vessels) *hae lang lugs*. Those who drink too much often say too much.

- M -

MAWKIT

Scots is rich in words relating to dirt and one of these words is *mawkit*. Now there is dirt and there is dirt and *mawkit* lies at the filthy end of the dirt scale. *Mawkit*, commonly also spelt *maukit* and sometimes *mockit*, is a two-syllable word pronounced as it is spelt with the emphasis on the first syllable which rhymes with "law".

There is often more than a hint of exaggeration in the use of *mawkit*. People and things so described may not be quite as dirty as the word suggests. *Mawkit* is often used of children and certainly, even in these days of over-protection, some children have a propensity to get absolutely filthy. They can rightly be described as *mawkit*. However, a few smears of chocolate on the face and white shirt do not really merit the use of *mawkit*.

Similarly, houses and cars have been known to be described as *mawkit* when really all they are in need of is a bit of a wipe. *Mawkitness*, like beauty and so many other things, is in the eyes of the beholder.

Given its meaning, *mawkit* is obviously anything but a pleasant word and, appropriately, its background is far from pleasant. It is derived from *mawk* which came to Scots from Middle English, and probably has its origins in Old Norse. A *mawk*, or *mauk*, is a maggot.

For the sake of those unfamiliar with maggots, they are soft, pale-coloured, worm-like things which are the larvae of flies. They are often to be found in rotting meat and other unsavoury things. They also inhabit corpses which have been left lying around and this gets them a mention in a lot of crime fiction these days. Apparently, forensic scientists can date the time that has elapsed since the death of the corpse by assessing the stage of development of the maggots in the corpse. Gruesome, but true!

Rotting meat and abandoned corpses can literally be described as *mawkit*. *Mawk*, as well as being a noun meaning a maggot, can be a verb meaning to infest with maggots. In English the past tense and past participle of regular verbs is formed with the ending 'ed', but in Scots this often becomes 'it'. Thus *mawkit* literally means infested with maggots. Sheep are apparently martyrs to this problem when they get maggots embedded in their flesh. Yet they just stand in their fields grazing on stoically.

MESSAGES

The average UK high street has changed enormously over recent decades. Now high streets tend to be a sea of charity shops interspersed with a series of take-aways and a few empty shops. Occasionally the odd small shop will remain to remind us what high streets used to be like in their glory days.

For example, most high streets used to have small grocery shops, butchers, fish shops and so on. These were the places that people used to *go the messages*. This Scottish expression is not as common as it once was, but then the shopping experience which it describes has practically disappeared.

To *go the messages* is to go and shop for everyday goods, such as foodstuffs. In the days when the expression was popular people, mostly women because these were sexist times, often did their food shopping either literally every day or, at least, very frequently. There were no giant freezers or fridges in the kitchen and storage space was often at a premium. Then there was the fact that food tended to go off more rapidly in the days before we introduced so many additives and preservatives to the food we eat.

Using a verb of motion, go, was obviously appropriate since shopping for the family involved moving from shop to shop, grocers to butchers, butchers to bakers and so on. Clearly this could take quite a lot of time, especially since the shoppers almost certainly lingered for a good old gossip in each shop. How unlike today's weekly or monthly frenzied race round the supermarket spent throwing into the trolley things that might well end up unused a few weeks later.

Going the messages, or, alternatively, *doing the messages*, usually involved the use of a sturdy shopping bag, known, not surprisingly, as a *message bag*, This was often literally a bag for life, even sometimes spanning more than one generation. Nowadays, this would be hailed as a great contribution to the conservation of the environment, since, of course, it was not made of plastic and could be readily disposed of, if you so chose. There again, the environment was not under such a threat in those days.

Those who were too frail or too lazy to lug the messages themselves could always rely on the *message boy*, known in English as an *errand boy*, to deliver the goods. The *message boy*, whistling along merrily on what was sometimes called, not very imaginatively, *a message bike* was the forerunner of online shopping. Again, he was environmentally-friendly and perhaps we should consider bringing him back. Not only would this help to save the environment, but it would provide some well-needed youth employment. I doubt if being a message boy paid very much, but it would have been more lucrative than work experience and I am sure there were a few tips to be had.

Message is not always associated in Scots with shopping. If you are asked to *go a message* for someone you have been selected to perform a task for someone that involves going from point A to point B, or even further. The purpose varies. You might have to deliver an invitation, pick up a prescription from the chemist, put on a bet at the bookies and so on.

The English equivalent of go a message is *run an errand*. The element of motion remains, but the speed of the motion is faster. For example, someone might ask a neighbour's child to run a few errands for them, hopefully giving the said child a suitable reward. It seems to me that running errands is more common in American English these days than it is in British English. However, Americans often seem to drop the idea of motion and talk of *taking care of a few errands* instead. Perhaps all this running has worn them out.

Scots shares with English the sense of *message* meaning a piece of communication, usually quite brief, left for a person who is absent or out of contact. In both languages *message* is ultimately derived from Latin *missus*, past participle of the verb *mittere*, to send.

Of course, *message* in the communication sense has moved with the times. Nowadays it is very likely to be electronic in nature. If we are *doing our messages* today we are more likely to be checking and sending emails than we are to be out shopping for food.

MIDDEN

The word *midden* in both Scots and English originally meant a pile of animal waste as found in a farmyard, otherwise known as a dunghill. The word originated in Old Norse and came to us from Middle English *myddyng*.

In both Scots and English *midden* then came to mean a pile of rubbish generally. The word still exists in English, but it is generally regarded either as rather old-fashioned or archaic or dialectal. This did not happen

Favourite Scots Words

in Scotland where *midden* has gone from strength to strength. From being a rubbish tip, a compost heap or a domestic ash-pit, *midden* came to mean a bin for refuse, or dustbin, and its contents. In some places it was used to refer to the area at the back of tenements where communal dustbins were kept. *Midden* kept pace with developments in sanitation and came to be used to describe the domestic rubbish put out for collection by the relevant local authority.

What is often now known as *bin day*, the day on which refuse is collected, was frequently known as *midden day*. Of course, in these days of recycling there are often several *midden days* in the week, one for cardboard, one for glass and so on.

The *bin lorry* (I am not sure what the current politically correct official term for that is) in some parts of Scotland was known as the *midden motor*. Another name for this was *midgie motor* and this was manned by *midgie men*.

A *midden raker*, also *midgie raker*, was someone who went through other people's rubbish in the hope of finding something that they found useful or valuable. If the raker was female she was known as a *midden mavis*. The modern equivalent of *midden rakers* are to be found driving round skips. *Middens* where the most valuable discarded items were likely to be found, mostly in areas where the rich lived, were known as *lucky middens*.

Midden can be used figuratively of either a place or a person. A kitchen that is in need of a good clean can rightly be described as a *midden*, as can a car that is full of assorted sweet wrappings, crisp packets, juice cartons, decaying banana skins and less savoury objects. A *knacker's midden* is an extreme example of either of these. A person dubbed a *midden* is also often in need of a good clean or at least a rigorous tidy up. Alternatively, a *midden* can be a particularly greedy person or animal.

The *midden heid* literally refers to the top of a dunghill, but figuratively it can be used to indicate a person's home territory or environment. A *middenstead* is the site of a *midden* or, figuratively, a person's usual haunt or stamping ground.

Midden has brought us some expressive idioms. If you are described *as either in the moon or the midden* you fluctuate between two extremes of mood. Should *you look at the moon till you fall in the midden* you have let yourself be carried away by your dreams and ambitions until you are brought back to earth with a bump to face harsh reality. To *marry a midden*

Favourite Scots Words

for its muck has nothing to do with hitching yourself to an unhygienic person, but means to marry someone for their money and disregard any other considerations.

I said above that *midden* in English is generally regarded as being archaic or dialectal. However, there is one notable exception. *Midden* has a specific archaeological sense which is still current in English. Often known as *kitchen midden*, this *midden* refers to the site of an old tip or dump for domestic waste, such as bone, fragments of pottery, shells, artefacts and so on, discarded by our ancestors of long ago at their settlements. Apparently, there is much to be learned about their lives, habits and diets from *kitchen middens*. I wonder what future archaeologists will make of our landfill sites.

MINGIN

Many of our Scots words stay right at home, but some escape into the wider world. For example, **dreich** referring to the weather is occasionally used by people south of the border, often in rather a self-conscious way as though they were enclosing it in air quotes. *Mingin,* pronounced as it is spelt, is another escapee, but this Scots word is unusual in having found a place in modern slang. It comes from the Scots verb *ming,* meaning to give off such a strong and unpleasant smell that it makes you want to hold your nose.

In Scots a piece of meat that has long since passed its use-by-date can be *mingin,* as can an overflowing dustbin urgently in need of emptying or a fridge full of long-forgotten left-overs. If *mingin* is used of a person in Scots, the person in question is usually badly in need of some soap and water and a change of clothes.

Mingin in English slang is much wider in meaning and there is often no suggestion of having a bad smell literally. I first encountered this wider meaning in Scotland in the mid-1980s. It was used of a teacher by the friend of one of my children. Since I had met that particular teacher and had not noticed his need of a strong anti-perspirant, I inquired of the meaning. The answer was that the teacher was simply no good.

In the slang sense *mingin* can be used to mean, for example, disgusting, of poor quality, unpleasant or unattractive. So, food can be *mingin,* a pub can be *mingin,* the weather can be *mingin,* a member of the opposite sex can be

Favourite Scots Words

mingin. In fact, people quite often use the word just to indicate their acute dislike or disapproval of someone or something.

Mingin was adopted with great enthusiasm by the "yoof" culture throughout the UK as rather a nasty term of insult and it has shown remarkable staying power. When I come across such expressions as *mingin chav* or, worse, *mingin minger* I cannot help feeling that *mingin* would have been better to stay at home.

Incidentally, *mingin* in Scots can also mean drunk. We have quite a few words for that state in Scots.

MUCKLE

Muckle is now best known to most people for its appearance in the old adage *Mony a mickle maks a muckle*. This is popularly thought to mean that a lot of small amounts of something will make a large amount of it. It is often used to try and encourage people to save little amounts of money in the hope, one day, that these will become a fortune.

The sentiment may be admirable, but the saying as it stands actually does not make much sense. *Mickle* and *muckle*, far from being opposites in meaning, actually mean the same thing. As nouns they both mean a large amount or a great deal of something. As adjectives they both mean large or great in size. Many Scots words have variations in spelling and *muckle/mickle* is an example. *Meikle* is another variation of the same word, as in *the meikle stane* (stone) mentioned in Tam o' Shanter, the well-known narrative poem by Robert Burns:

> *And past the birks and meikle stane,*
>
> *Where drunken Charlie brak's neck-bane.*

How the saying *Mony a mickle maks a muckle* came about is a bit of a mystery. The most likely explanation is that the phrase started out life *as Mony a pickle maks a muckle*. *Pickle*, unlike *mickle*, is opposite in meaning to *muckle* and means a small amount. This phrase, then, has the merit of making sense. If that is the case, a most unlikely person appears to have been involved in the faulty rewording of the saying. That person is George Washington. In 1793 he referred in writing to a Scots saying "many mickles make a muckle" adding "than which nothing in nature is more true". I doubt if he single-handedly caused the *mickle* problem, but he certainly added to it.

Favourite Scots Words

Mony a mickle maks a muckle might be linguistically inaccurate, but it has spread its wings further into England than most Scots words and phrases have done. To add to the confusion, a version of the saying has appeared in some English dialects as *Many a little makes a mickle*.

The word *muckle* is derived from Old English *micel*, meaning great or large, which is associated with Old Norse *mikill* of the same meaning. *Muckle* can be used as a noun, as in the saying under discussion, or as in They dinna think muckle o' him, used to emphasize a poor opinion of someone. However, *muckle* is often used as an adjective in a wide range of contexts, as in a *muckle* tree, a *muckle* hoose, a *muckle* difference, a *muckle* eejit (idiot) and so on.

Muckle feck refers to the larger or lion's share of something, *muckle coat* to a greatcoat and *muckle chair* to a particularly large armchair. The *muckle tae* is the big toe and the town of Langholm in Dumfriesshire is frequently known as the *Muckle Toon*.

Muckle is also found in compound adjectives such as *muckle-moued*, having an exceptionally large mouth. *Muckle-backit* means having a good strong back, always an asset, and *muckle-boukit*, in one of its senses, means having a large powerful physique. In its other sense it means pregnant, hardly a flattering description of a mother-to-be.

Muckle has extended its senses to mean adult or grown up. Thus an expression such as someone's *muckle dochter* can be ambiguous. She can either be a large (probably not a compliment) daughter or a grown-up daughter. Muckle can also mean high-ranking or important, as in the *muckle fowk* (people).

Muckle fowk have often achieved their *muckledom* by being wealthy. This reminds me of another *muckle* saying---*Moyen* (influence) *does muckle, but money does mair* (more). How true!

- N -

Neep *see under* **Tumshie**

Nyaff

Those of you who regularly use insults and have grown weary of **bauchle** might consider turning to *nyaff* for a change. *Nyaff*, which is pronounced as it is spelt, with the y being sounded as a consonant like the y in "yoke", can be used, like *bauchle*, as a general term of insult. Anyone who gets on your nerves, anyone of whom you wildly disapprove or anyone whom you consider to be worthless or good-for-nothing, can be described as a *nyaff*.

However, the use of this insult was originally restricted to a small, puny and generally insignificant person, especially one who was conceited and impudent and given to senseless chatter. It could also be applied to a spoilt, bad-mannered child. When it was used of things, it meant something small of its kind, often something of little or no value.

Nyaff could also be used to describe the impudent, cheeky talk of a forward child. In addition, it could be used to refer to the yapping or yelping of a small dog. This could have something to do with the derivation of the insult. In origin, the word *nyaff* may be imitative of the noise made by an excitable small dog, such as a terrier.

The word *nyaff* started life off as a verb. It had several meanings, including to chatter meaninglessly on, to harp on about something, or to snap at each other when arguing. Used of a small dog, it meant to yelp or yap. Rarer meanings include to work ineffectually without making much effort, to be idle or to waste time. It could also mean to walk with very short steps.

There are some adjectives that *nyaff* seems to attract and you can use these to add emphasis or strength to your original insult. One of these is **shilpit** which shares with *nyaff* suggestions of physical weakness and lack of stature. The other is **shauchlin.**

- O -

OOSE

I am a lifelong member of the Quentin Crisp school of housework. Like him, I firmly believe that "after the first four years the dirt doesn't get any worse."

So it is that on those occasions when I have to pull out a bed to see if some lost object has rolled underneath it, I regularly encounter piles of *oose*. "Piles of what?" I hear you cry, possibly hopeful that I am being rude.

I am not. I am simply using the Scots word to describe that greyish, dusty, woolly tangled stuff that gathers under beds which have been left undisturbed for some time. I tend to spell this word *oose*, but it can also be spelt *ooze*, *oos*, or *ooss*. Scots, having no official standard spelling, is the perfect language for those whose knowledge of spelling is a bit hazy. Pronounced to rhyme with "loose", *oose* is derived from oo, the Scots word for wool.

By now, you will probably have worked out that members of the English-speaking world know this word as *fluff*. *Oose* is a far more descriptive word than *fluff* and some of you might well fall in love with it and plan to use it.

A word of warning. *Oose* and *fluff* are not completely interchangeable That young blonde on that wealthy-looking elderly man's arm may be his bit of *fluff*. However, she is not his bit of *oose*.

In any case, give him the benefit of the doubt. She could really be his niece.

ORRA

It is almost impossible these days to avoid some form of sales communication even in the privacy of your own home. Either you are being harassed at meal times by a constant stream of so-called courtesy calls or you are being inundated by reams of leaflets offering a myriad of goods and services. Recently, I seem to have been targeted by leaflets from people calling themselves handymen, a result no doubt of growing unemployment.

Handymen are also known as *odd job men* and in Scots they can be known as *orramen*. The word *orraman* was very familiar to me as a child because I was brought up in the country and *orramen* were particularly common on farms. Urban dwellers would be less likely to encounter the word. The work carried out by an *orraman*, or, indeed, by an *orrawoman*, *orra laddie* or *orra lassie* (for there was nothing sexist or ageist about *orra*), was known as *orra work*.

The adjective *orra*, pronounced as it is spelt, with the first syllable rhyming with the word "for", is of uncertain origin. It is thought that it may be a shortened form of *ower a*, (ower being pronounced, roughly speaking, to rhyme with "our"), meaning over all.

Orra has a variety of meanings. In relation to *orra work* and the people engaged in this, the word means casual or unskilled. *Orra* can also be used of someone who is unemployed or who has nothing useful to do.

It can also be applied to a place or building that is unused or unoccupied or has no one particular use. Thus, an *orra shed* can be used for housing hens, storing logs and garden implements, keeping bikes and so on.

Something that is surplus to requirements can be described as *orra*. A spare bed that can be put at the disposal of a visitor can be called *orra* as can, for example, a basket of apples from an over-abundant crop that is given to a neighbour.

One of the several meanings of *orra* is miscellaneous. The contents of a garden shed, boy's pocket or junk shop can all be described as *orra*. Most *orra* of the lot is the motley collection of things to be found in the depths of the average woman's handbag.

Orra shares some of the meanings of the English word *odd*. For example, one of a pair of things that is without its partner, such as the sock that mysterious loses its mate in the washing machine, is called *odd* in English, but *orra* in Scots. In Scots *orra*, used of a woman, used to mean that she was unmarried.

Orra, like *odd*, can also mean occasional or happening at infrequent intervals. Thus, visitors to somewhere might be an uncommon occurrence, but an *orra body* or the *odd person* might come along now and then and relieve the monotony.

Both *orra body* and *odd person* can also be used to refer to someone who is considered strange, uncommon or abnormal. A person who wears strange clothes, talks to themselves or otherwise acts in an eccentric or idiosyncratic way that is unacceptable to the masses, can be described as *orra*. To be described as *orra* in the sense of strange or abnormal is not exactly a compliment, but *orra* can be used to suggest even more undesirable qualities. *Orra*, when used of a person, can mean worthless, shabby, slovenly, coarse and disreputable. It can also be used of things, such as clothes, to mean shabby or worn out.

Be sure not to confuse this *orra* with the *orra* in the informal Scots greeting *orra best* (all the best).

OXTER

I was completely laden the other day after a trip to the shops. Bags hung from both hands and both shoulders and I had to resort to carrying things under my *oxter*. Where?

The English word for *oxter* is *armpi*t-- by no stretch of the imagination a pleasant word. Unfortunately, pit immediately suggests a deep dark place where something nameless may be festering. This may be quite an apt description of some old-style under-arm areas, particularly those belonging to the male of the species, but there has been a transformation. Nowadays, this area has, in many cases, become a silky smooth, sweet-smelling area with no unpleasant surprises even on some male bodies. It is no longer the pits.

Armpit may no longer be a suitable name for this new-style sanitized under-arm area, but will *oxter* be adopted by a wider public to replace it? Almost certainly not. Unlike many Scots words, the word *oxter* is not a particularly descriptive word and it is not a particularly charming one.

Oxter may lack obvious charm, but it is a very useful word. It can be used to stress how busy you are, for you can be *up to your oxters* in all manner of activities. At least it makes a change from ears.

Oxter can act as a verb and so you can find someone, or possibly two people, *oxtering* someone else home. Perhaps the someone else has had a few drinks too many and is in need of a helping arm.

Oxter also features in several phrases. One of my favourites is *wi yir heid under yir oxter* translated literally as "with your head under your armpit". Figuratively it means downcast or depressed, but do not try this at home.

- P -

PAN LOAF

More and more people across the world are learning English as a foreign or second language. It is one of the few growth industries. Many of these learners become very proficient in the language and so, when they visit Britain, they find it very easy to make themselves understood. They may find it surprising, though, to find out that it is not always so easy to understand what the locals are saying in reply.

Although the UK is geographically quite small in size, linguistically there are many variations from region to region. The learner will probably have learnt RP, or Received Pronunciation, supposedly proper English as spoken by those at the upper end of the English social and educational scales, especially originally those in the area around London. However, the vast majority of native speakers do not speak in that way.

Visitors to Scotland will experience several different forms of pronunciation as they travel through the country. Some of them at least will almost certainly encounter the form of speech known as *pan loaf*. This is the name given not to an accent that is native to any particular region, but to a very affected way of speaking used by people who wish to seem ultra-refined and to appear to be a few rungs further up the social ladder than they actually are. They affect this style of speech in order to impress others, but, of course, they very often achieve the opposite effect and end up being ridiculed.

Talking *pan loaf* has its origins in a type of bread. A *pan loaf* refers to a loaf that is baked individually in a pan or tin and has a thin, smooth crust all round it. This contrasts with a plain loaf which has crust just on the top and bottom, the crust on top being darker and harder, and is baked in batches. *Pan loaves* were more expensive and were thought to be favoured by more genteel eaters some of whom were likely to speak *pan loaf* or *pan loafy*, as it is sometimes known.

Pan in Scots shares some of the meanings of the word in English, especially a cooking vessel of some kind. The word is Old English in origin and has linguistic connections with German *pfanne*, Dutch *pan* and Swedish *panna*.

Staying with the cooking theme, we have *pancakes* in both Scotland and

Favourite Scots Words

England, but they are different in form. The *pancake* cooked in Scotland, like the one cooked in England, is a round flat cake made with batter. However, the Scots one is much smaller and thicker than the English one. In England the Scots *pancake* is sometimes known as a *drop scone* or *Scotch pancake*.

Those with a sweet tooth like to put loads of jam on pancakes. Those with an even sweeter tooth like to sook (=suck) another Scottish pan favourite, a *pan drop*. This is a type of hard round white mint sweet traditionally loved by old ladies and used as a breath-sweetener by people who wish to hide the fact that they have been drinking alcohol. Beware. People with too sweet a tooth can be rendered toothless by overindulging in these.

On a more savoury note, there is *pan jotral*, also found in the plural form. This refers to leftovers or to odds and ends of food of the kind that lie around in your fridge. The term originally referred to a dish made from the offal of slaughtered animals, or to such offal itself. The thought of that makes me feel rather squeamish and so I will move swiftly on.

In Scots *pan* can also be used to refer to the skull or cranium. If you are of a violent turn of mind, and perhaps seeking vengeance on someone, you might threaten to *knock their pan in*. You can also *knock your pan in* and become completely exhausted.

PAWKIE

Family sledging can be one of the delights of winter, but there can be a downside. If you have young children it takes forever to get them dressed warmly enough to withstand the ravages of the cold and snow. When you finally get to the slope they complain about snow going down their wellingtons and their hands being cold and declare that they want to go home. Their hands are cold often because they have refused to wear gloves or *pawkies* or have taken them off.

For the information of the uninitiated, *pawkies* is a Scots word for gloves without individual finger coverings, only an individual covering for the thumb and one large one for all the rest of the fingers. In English they are called *mitts* or *mittens*.

They have the merit of being easier to put on a child's hands than traditional gloves. However, it is practically impossible to manoeuvre or manipulate anything while you are wearing them. Thus, they are even more likely than gloves to be divested by children.

The item that the word *pawkie* is used to describe is still in common use. Not so the word itself, I fear. Most of the people I have come across who know the word are, like myself, a bit long in the tooth. This is a pity because, to me, the word *pawkie* has far more character than *mitt* or *mitten*.

Like many words, both Scots and English, *pawkie* is of uncertain origin. It has been suggested that it comes from the word *paw* with the addition of endings *–ock* and *–ie*, both of which can be used to create diminutive forms. (Note, however, that while a hillock is a small hill, a postie is not necessarily a small postman.)

I may have confused some of you with this use of *pawkie*. It is more commonly found as an adjective with a completely different meaning, unconnected to the glove meaning. In this sense *pawkie*, which has the alternative and very common spelling *pawky*, can mean wily, shrewd or resourceful. It can also mean having a dry, rather sardonic sense of humour, a style of humour which is held to be common among Scots.

Pawkie also has some less well-known meanings. It can be used to refer to a task that is particularly difficult to carry out. It can also be applied to a task which has to be done with exceptional care or to one which requires some kind of special knowledge.

There is a lighter side to *pawkie*. It can mean lively, merry or vivacious. Thus, you can set out to the office Christmas party in *pawkie* mood. Alternatively, *pawkie* can be rather saucy and refer to someone or something that it is a bit coquettish or even wanton. Beware those *pawkie* glances from the girl standing under the mistletoe if you are already spoken for.

Pawkie has even more strings to its bow. It can mean quaint or fantastic and it can be used critically to refer to someone who is smug, proud or vain. Lots to choose from there and plenty of room for ambiguity.

PECH

Edinburgh is a city that is noted for its natural beauty, its historical buildings and its annual Festival. Visitors regularly flock to it. Many of them have remembered to pack appropriate weather-wear, having been forewarned of the city's uncertain climate. But, as one woman said to me the other day, nobody warns visitors about the hilly streets.

Favourite Scots Words

She could have a point. Certainly it is true that a trip to some of the Festival venues will leave the less fit among the visitors red of face and *peching*. Dedicated couch potatoes may be close to collapse.

To *pech* in Scots means to breathe heavily, usually after taking exercise. The English equivalent is *pant*, but this is not nearly so descriptive. The breathy sound of *pech* more eloquently describes the person left almost gasping for breath. Indeed, the word *pech* probably came into being because the sound of it so aptly echoes the meaning.

The *ch* in *pech* is pronounced like the *ch* of "loch", not the *ch* of "much". For those of you not familiar with the correct pronunciation of loch, try the *ch* in the composer *Bach*.

The verb *pech* can also refer to the process of walking, getting about, working, etc, when this involves more exertion than the body cares for or is up to. Thus, you may find some occasional Sunday afternoon ramblers "*peching* up a hill" when the more experienced and fleet of foot trip effortlessly past them.

Pech can also mean to cough in a wheezy way, as though you were asthmatic. It can also refer to letting the breath out slowly and loudly, as when sighing with satisfaction or relief or when groaning. Apparently it can be used figuratively to mean to have an ardent desire for, although to "*pech* for the embrace of a loved one" sounds far from romantic.

Pech can also act as a noun. If you are struggling to get your breath back after physical exertion you can be said to be *oot*(out) *o pech*, or *short o pech*. *Pech* can also be a wheezy, asthmatic cough or a sigh of weariness, satisfaction or relief.

The noun *pech* can also denote great effort, exertion or struggle. To get over something *wi a pech* is to get something done only by means of a tremendous effort. If something is *a sair* (sore) *pech* it requires prolonged and exhausting effort. This can refer to climbing a particularly steep hill – but, for many, life itself can be *a sair pech*. What a cheery thought for the day!

PEELIE-WALLY

Many of us who have a Celtic genetic inheritance have very fair skin.

Usually this creates no problems and a fair skin can be a decided beauty asset. Pale skin looks fine against a background of its native heath, but transfer it to a sun-baked foreign beach and things change dramatically. Pale skin can stand out like an unfortunate sore thumb when surrounded by a sea of bronzed bodies. The Scots word *peelie-wally* springs to mind.

Peelie-wally, also spelt *peelie-wallie* and with *wally* pronounced to rhyme with "sally", can mean *pale*, but in this sense it is far from being a compliment. You might describe a flawless porcelain complexion as *pale*, but you are very unlikely to describe it as *peelie-wally*. Rather, *peelie-wally* means pallid or washed-out looking, like the odd pale body among a multitude of sun-tanned ones.

Peelie-wally is often used to refer to the kind of paleness that accompanies ill health. If a child is looking *peelie-wally* it is often a sign of impending sickness of some kind. In fact, *peelie-wally* can mean ill-looking or sickly or, by extension, thin or feeble.

Things as well as people can be described as *peelie-wally* when something colourless or insipid is being referred to. For example, you might refer to the beige décor of someone's house as *peelie-wally* if you are the sort of person who prefers strong colours. Or you might criticize the pastel colours of someone's dress as being too *peelie-wally*. If you like a strong cup of tea you might describe a weaker form of the beverage as *peelie-wally*.

An activity or performance of some kind can also be referred to as *peelie-wally* when it lacks vigour or vitality. Not surprisingly, this use usually occurs in connection with Scotland's obsession with football. Apparently there are many instances of *peelie-wally* performances on the pitch.

The expression *peelie-wally* started life out simply as *peelie*. This is likely to have a connection with the Scots word *palie* meaning sickly, listless, delicate or stunted in growth and *palie* is, in turn, likely to be connected with English *pale*.

However, it has been suggested that the origin of the *peelie* of *peelie-wally* may be imitative of a kind of whining, feeble noise made by people who are ill. As for the *wally*, it may just have been added for effect and may have been influenced by the Scots word *paewae* meaning pallid, sickly or insipid. The suggestion that there is a connection with the whiteness of *wallie*, meaning china or porcelain, seems less likely. But back to our sun-baked beach. There is good news for the *peelie-wally*. Now that over-exposure to the sun is known to cause major skin problems, official health advice is to cover up in the sun. There is now no need to reveal yourself in all your *peelie-wally* glory on the beach. In any case, the *peelie-wally* skin does not bronze. It just goes an unattractive shade of red.

PEERIE

Peerie has two different meanings in Scots. One of these relates to dimensions and means small. This meaning of *peerie*, although formerly more widespread, is now most common in Orkney and Shetland. Like many words its origin is doubtful, although it is thought to have connections with Norwegian dialect *piren*, meaning thin, feeble, sickly or niggardly and Swedish dialect *pirug*, meaning slender or little.

Peerie in this sense has given rise to a number of interesting phrases. You might possibly think that *peerie folk* are children. This is quite logical, children being small people, but it is not correct. *Peerie folk* are even smaller than children. They are fairies.

The expression *peerie breeks* sounds as though it might be used to describe trousers or knickers that are too tight and literally, this would be the case. Figuratively, however, someone referred to a *peerie breeks* is either a small child or, more insultingly, a person who is vertically challenged and has exceptionally short legs.

The other meaning of *peerie* is probably better known. Primarily, it means a child's spinning top. Other meanings include a fir cone and a small stone marble. The spinning top in question was spun into motion by a string known as a *peerie cord* or *peerie string*.

This meaning of *peerie* has also given us some interesting phrases. The one that a good few of you are likely to have come across is *peerie heels*. These are high, sharply-pointed heels which appear on women's fashionable shoes. In more modern parlance they are known as stiletto heels or, when they reach new heights of discomfort, *killer heels*. They are a podiatrist's dream because they cause so many foot problems to wearers in later life.

To *sleep like a peerie* is the direct equivalent of English to *sleep like a top*. Both expressions mean to sleep exceptionally soundly, which may seem rather odd. Since a *peerie* or top goes round and round all the time you might think that to sleep like either a *peerie* or a *top* meant to sleep fitfully, constantly tossing and turning. However, apparently in top terminology sleep means to spin steadily and smoothly without wobbling. You learn something new everyday!

The expression *peerie-heedit* does not mean that you have a head shaped like a top. It means that your head feels as though it is spinning round and round all the time like a top, indicating a state of deep confusion. This is often caused by having too many things to do and too little time to do them in, the modern disease in fact.

As to origin, *peerie* might well be derived from the Scots word *peer*, the equivalent of the English fruit, *pear*. After all, you could describe tops as being pear-shaped in that they have a rounded bottom part and a narrower top part.

Of course, today it is not usually tops that are described as *pear-shaped*. The expression is mostly reserved for either people's bodies or things that go horribly wrong. I wonder if you would feel better any about such a disastrous situation if you called it *peerie-shaped*. Probably not!

PERJINK

Words relating to neatness and orderliness seem to be much thinner on the ground in Scots than words relating to grubbiness. However, we can rely on the word *perjink* to show that we are not entirely a nation of slovens.

Perjink is a crisp, neat-sounding word and this points the way to its meaning. Usually used of a person, it means neat, tidy, or smart. I often think of it as another word for the English word *dapper*, but that is too restrictive. *Dapper* is mostly used with reference to a man while *perjink* is definitely unisex. Carefully-groomed, well-turned out women have as much right as men to be described as *perjink*.

In this sense, *perjink* is obviously a compliment, but the word has a downside. It can also be used as a term of criticism or insult. For example, it can be used to refer to people who are rather priggish, prim or strait-laced. They have become so concerned with the neatness of their appearance that they have lost all sense of spontaneity.

Perjink can also mean extremely careful or very exact or precise, the sort of qualities that may be considered admirable in an accountant. In this sense, it means much the same as the English word *meticulous* and the two words also share a less flattering meaning. They can both be used to refer to someone who has gone over the top when practising care and precision, especial over trivial details, and ended up fussy, finicky or nit-picking.

Favourite Scots Words

Such a person can also be described as *pernicketie* or *pernickety*. It may surprise you to know that this has its origin in the Scots language, which is known for its flexibility in spelling. Later, it was adopted into English, where it is usually spelt pernickety. Where would they be without us?

Pernickety *see under* **Perjink**.

PINKIE

What do you call the smallest slender finger on your hand? If you are a Scot who has been properly brought up you will instantly reply *"pinkie"*. People who hesitate before giving an answer may actually use the word *pinkie*, but may be reluctant to admit it. This is because they think that use of the diminutive word *pinkie* sounds like something that they should have left behind in childhood.

Not a bit of it. *Pinkie* is a perfectly respectable grown-up word Scots word. Furthermore, its use is not restricted to Scots. *Pinkie* is also found in American English, not just in those parts where Scots settled in large numbers, but throughout the States.

The word *pinkie* is a bit of a cosmopolitan. Not only does it have American associations, but it has dallied with the Dutch. In origin, it is connected with Dutch *pink*, which also refers to the smallest finger.

If Scots and Americans both use the word *pinkie* what do English speakers say? They use the much more boring expression little finger or sometimes small finger. My problem with both of these is that I simply cannot take them seriously. For some reason they both conjure up a ridiculous picture of an ultra-genteel lady daintily drinking tea out of a china cup with her little finger raised in the air. This pose used to be considered an essential part of tea-drinking etiquette for ladies. Perhaps it still is. I don't move in these circles. I drink my tea out of a mug.

There will be Scots around who use neither *pinkie* nor *little finger*, but who prefer *wee finger*. In this case *finger* is pronounced in the Scots way to rhyme with "singer", not in the English way to rhyme with "linger".

There was a Battle of Pinkie in 1547. This conflict between the Scots and the English had nothing whatsoever to do with small fingers, but took its name from the site of the battle, near Musselburgh. It was a famous victory—but not, alas, for the Scots.

Favourite Scots Words

- R -

Reek *see under* **Rift**.

RIFT

The English word *belch* does not sound at all discreet. This is fair enough. The action it describes is not at all discreet either. Expelling air from your stomach loudly through your mouth, whether accidentally or deliberately, is bound to draw attention to you.

To me, the Scots word *rift* does sound rather discreet, although it actually describes the same in-your-face action as *belch*. Somehow it conjures up a picture of someone politely trying to suppress the full blast of the sound, perhaps behind a strategically placed hand.

But this is fancy on my part. To *rift* is but to *belch* and a *rift* is a *belch*. The word *rift*, which was first recorded in the middle of the 15th century, has come down to us via Middle English from Old Norse *rypta*.

At one point in its history *rift* could describe wind being expelled from either end, not just the mouth. I have seen expelling wind from the nether end described as "to break wind backwards". Now there is a discreet expression! The poet Allan Ramsay makes reference to this sense of *rift* in his *Collection of Scots Proverbs* (1736). "It is a sign of a hale heart to rift at the rumple" goes the proverb. *Rumple* in Scots is a word for the buttocks.

Belching is said to be a way of conveying your compliments to the chef in certain cultures. I am not sure whether *riftin* ever had the same interpretation in Scotland, but *riftin fou* (rifting full) means completely full up, suggesting that the consumer had enjoyed the food.

The verb *to rift* had the additional meaning of to brag or to exaggerate your achievements, success etc, and this gave rise to the adjective *rifty*, overly wordy. To *rift oot* once meant to emit through the mouth as if belching and this applied particularly to the issuing of threats.

To *rift up* described regurgitated food coming back up into the mouth, as when belching. Figuratively, this phrase could be used of something that you would rather forget coming back into your mind to haunt you, a regurgitated memory so to speak.

Rift can also function as a noun with meanings corresponding to that of the verb. Thus, *rift* can be an act of belching and *brunt rift* refers to that painful condition known in English as heartburn. To *hae* (have) *the rift o* describes the unpleasant experience of having food repeating on you. This is even worse if the food was not to your taste first time round.

The noun *rift* can also refer to a piece of unsubstantiated bragging or to rather verbose flowery language. If you're indulging in a good old lively chat, that can also be a *rift*.

A more formal or technical English equivalent of *rift* is *eructate*. I mention this, partly to show off and partly to have an excuse to mention another Scots word.

Eructate is derived from the Latin verb *ructare*, to spew out. It has been suggested that this may have some connection with Scots **reek** and related words from other northern languages, such as German *rauch*. Scots for smoke, *reek* is something that is spewed or belched out of a chimney, as opposed to out of a body orifice.

RUNKLE

Of all the tedious household tasks, I dislike ironing the most. Yet I have friends who actually find pleasure in it and claim to find it a soothing occupation. I find iron irritating rather than calming, and cannot really see the point of removing *runkles* from things that will immediately acquire other *runkles* as soon as they are worn or used.

A *runkle* is Scots for *crease*. Like many Scots words, it is much more descriptive than its English equivalent, especially when applied to something that is seriously crushed and crumpled. *Crease* is rather a genteel-sounding word, while *runkle* suggests a more corrugated effect. I never iron anything unless the garment or other object in question has reached the seriously corrugated stage.

Runkle can also be used to describe a *wrinkle*, such as those that are to be found on the faces of those who no longer have the bloom of youth or who have spent too long in the sun. I personally would not use it in this sense, although I would always use the word *runkle* instead of crease in relation to clothes etc. Facial *wrinkles* are just about acceptable and can, at a pinch, be called laughter lines. Facial *runkles*, on the other hand, suggest deep-set furrows that even serious cosmetic surgery can do nothing about.

Favourite Scots Words

Runkle can also be applied to a person and, as you might expect, it is hardly a compliment, being used to describe an old, wrinkled person. The English word *wrinklie*, also used to describe an ageing wrinkled person, is often labelled offensive, or something similar, in dictionaries. *Runklie*, however, would sound much more offensive.

Runkle can also be a verb. Thus, sitting around a lot can *runkle* clothes, particularly if they are made of linen. You can *runkle* your brow in deep thought or in anger or disapproval, but do not do this too often or you will end up with permanent *runkles*.

Runkle has given rise to the adjective *runkled*, as in *runkled* clothes, a *runkled* brow or, worse, a *runkled* face. It can also be used of something such as dry autumn leaves. The adjective *runkly*, meaning wrinkled, also exists.

Runkle is thought to be derived from Old Scandinavian *runkla*, to wrinkle. It has several Scandinavian linguistic cousins such as Danish *runken*, wrinkled, and Swedish *rynka*, wrinkle.

What help can be given to those non-ironers among us? Some people swear by hanging garments in the bathroom when you are taking a hot bath or shower so that steam will do the work of the iron in a painless way and remove, or at least reduce, *runkles*.

Or you can just live with the *runkles* and adopt the crumpled look. If you are a man some woman might take pity on you and offer to do your ironing. But not me.

- S -

SCUNNER

The Scots word *scunner* is associated with disgust or revulsion. Thus you can say that the sight of blood *scunners* you. If you are a vegetarian you might say that the smell of meat *scunners* you and I might say that the taste of cream of mushroom soup *scunners* me (it is one of my pet hates). The verb is often found in the passive and so you could say that you like lamb, but that you had so much of it on holiday that you are *scunnered* of it.

Scunner can also be associated with a less extreme reaction to something or someone and mean irritated, disapproving or disappointed. So a rejected candidate for a job might be heard to say he was *scunnered* at not getting the job. People can be *scunnered* when their football team loses once again (a seemingly common experience for some) or *scunnered* that it is teeming with rain on the one day that they were free to go to the beach. Many people are *scunnered* with their jobs, though dare not give them up, and many regularly get *scunnered* with the weather.

Scunner can also be used as a noun, with meanings corresponding to the verb, as in: "It's a real scunner that there's no direct train service there." A pregnant woman who is subject to sudden food cravings or aversions might remark that she has taken a real *scunner* to coffee.

You can *take a scunner* to someone whom you previously liked if they do something to irritate or upset you. Sometimes this process occurs just before you dump them.

People can also be referred to as *scunners*. You might accuse someone of being a *right scunner* for refusing to do as you wish to or just for arousing dislike or disapproval in you.

As is the case with so many words, the origin of *scunner* is unknown. The original meaning of the verb was more physical than its common meaning today. It meant to shrink back or flinch from someone or something. It is a small step from there to feeling revulsion.

Scunner has produced the adjectives *scunnerfu* and *scunnersome*, both meaning disgusting or nauseating. It has also given rise to *scunneration*, a noun used to refer to a particularly disgusting or offensive sight or to something that you particularly dislike. I once knew someone who used it

Favourite Scots Words

instead of a four-letter word to vent her feelings of anger, pain, etc when there were children present.

SCUTTER

Living near a beach as I do, I regularly witness happy, excited families parking their cars prior to carting to the beach all the requisite paraphernalia for a blissful day spent in the vicinity of sand, sea and sunscreen. Sadly, their return to their cars often demonstrates the downside of a family day out at the sea. Fractious, whining children and red parental faces, caused as often by frayed tempers as by too much sun, are frequently the order of the day. And then there is the prospect of the drive home!

Can it be worth it? Would not everyone be better off staying at home? The adults can knock back a few drinks while the children can *scutter* about in a paddling pool and sand pit in the back garden.

For those who get the general picture, but not the meaning of the word *scutter*, this is a Scots word, pronounced to rhyme with "butter" and having several meanings. In the particular context just given it means to splash about, often in a messy way, as children do in sandy paddling pools.

To *scutter* does not, by any means, always involve water, but it often involves mess, one way or the other. For example, you might say of rather a slapdash amateur cook "She offered to make dinner and spent most of the day scuttering about the kitchen leaving me to clean up after her."

Scuttering often involves a degree of bungling ineptness. Someone whose enthusiasm for tinkering with cars is considerably greater than his mechanical skills might spend years *scuttering about* with an old car trying to get it roadworthy without success. Still, as long as he is happy!

To *scutter* can also refer to spending time in pointless or time-wasting activities, to fiddle about with something, or to potter about. Thus, you could be accused of *scuttering about* on a Sunday morning when you have chosen to rearrange the contents of your box of pens instead of turning your attention to mowing the overgrown lawn. Students who are supposed to be studying for exams or writers facing a deadline are particularly prone to suffer from the urge to *scutter about*.

To *scutter* can also mean to detain or hinder someone from what they should be doing by bothering them with something unimportant. Thus, someone might scutter you by trying to force some totally irrelevant leaflets on you, thereby causing you to miss the bus.

Scutter can also be used as a noun. It can refer to the carrying out of a task in a botched, bungling, and often messy or slovenly, way. Alternatively, it can be used to describe a task that is time-consuming and footling, awkward or fiddly.

I was engaged in such a task recently when helping one of my grandchildren make a design with miniscule beads. Such a task merits the adjective *scutterie*. It was particularly *scutterie* as far as I was concerned since I am pretty well devoid of arts and crafts skills and have the added disadvantage of ageing fingers.

In common with a great many words, *scutter* is of uncertain origin. It has been suggested that it may be related to the English word *scuttle*. However, it has also been proposed that it may be an altered form of the Scots word *skitter*, meaning diarrhoea. Certainly the verb *skitter*, like *scutter*, can mean to waste time doing unimportant jobs.

Let us hope that the children on the beach or in the paddling pool do not *skitter* as well as *scutter*.

SEMMIT

If you cast a cloot before May was oot you may be in the process of redonning it because of the weather. What am I talking about? Most of you will know, but for the sake of the uninitiated I will tell you, that I am referring to a piece of sage advice – "ne'er cast a cloot till May be oot (out)."

Roughly speaking, this is a warning to people not to throw off their winter garments too soon on the assumption that summer has arrived. An argument has waged for decades over whether the "May" in question is the month or the hawthorn blossom, but I do not intend to get involved in this.

A *cloot* is a piece of cloth, but it can also, as here, be used of an article of clothing and the *cloot* referred to in the warning may well be a *semmit*. A *semmit* is a man's undershirt or vest, although *semmits* were once sometimes worn by women, and it was originally made of wool or flannel. The word is sometimes spelt *simmit* and its pronunciation often follows this second spelling, however it is spelt. Like so many words, *semmit* is of uncertain origin. The word *semat* appears in Old Scots in the 15th century referring to a Roman tunic but *semmit* or *semmet* is much later. It has been suggested that *semmet* may be a form of the English word *samite* meaning a fine silk cloth or a garment made of this. *Samite*, derived from old French, and sometimes interwoven with gold, was often used for ecclesiastical garments in the Middle Ages.

Samite sounds as though it was a cut above the *semmet* which was a fairly humble, basic garment and hardly stylish. Now of course such a garment can be made of materials other than scratchy wool or flannel. The *semmit* can be made of cotton or a man-made fabric, and perhaps even silk, and can come as part of a thermal winter package.

The problem is that, in this capacity, it has probably sloughed off the name *semmit* and become a vest. There is a price to be paid for becoming stylish. This is a pity. If we had stuck to *semmit* we would never had got caught up in the confusion between American and British English that exists with regard to *vest*.

In British English, *vest* is the equivalent of *semmit*. In American English a vest is a *waistcoat* and, in commercialese at least, this use has caught on in British English to some extent. Far better to stick to *semmit*. You know where you are with it and when to where it.

SHAUCHLIN

If the noun **nyaff** does not convey enough contempt for the person you wish to insult in Scots, you can always make it more vehement by preceding it with the word *wee* plus an adjective, such as **shilpit** or *shauchlin*, as in *shauchlin (or shauchlie) wee nyaff*.

Shauchlin, the first syllable of which is pronounced to rhyme with "loch", has various alternative forms, such as *shachlin, shauchlie* and *shachli*e. The word was originally used to describe a person's unsteady way of walking. A *shauchlin* person is someone who shuffles along without lifting their feet from the ground. Sometimes this is because they are wearing shoes that have seen considerably better days and so are difficult to walk in. In origin the word may be imitative of the sound made by someone shuffling.

Shauchlin can be used of objects other than shoes. When describing something such as a bike, a cart or a baby's buggy it means wobbly or rickety. By extension, it then came to be used of a person who was less than stable, someone who was not reliable and was considered to be generally unworthy, another useful insult.

Shauchlin, as you would expect, is derived from the verb *shauchle* meaning to shuffle or shamble along. It can also mean to wear something, such as shoes or garments, in such a way that they get distorted or twisted out of shape. *Shauchle* can also mean to shuffle or shake something off, to get rid of something. So, instead of shuffling off your mortal coil (as in Hamlet), you can *shauchle it aff* instead. Well, not just yet, I hope.

Shauchle also gives rise to *shauchled*. *Shauchled* shoes are shoes that are causing the wearer to shuffle or shamble along. They have been worn so much that they are out of shape and down at heel. It is small wonder, then, that the wearer is not exactly tripping lightly along.

Finally, *shauchle* can be a noun. It has several meanings, including a shuffling way of getting along, an old worn-out shoe or a weak, puny, stunted person (another insult). There are shades of **bauchle** here. A *bauchle* can mean an old worn out shoe that causes the wearer to shuffle along. We seem to have some kind of obsession with our feet when it comes to insults.

Shauchled shoes can be so worn that the only thing to do with them is to get rid of them. On analogy with this is a *shauchled* sweetheart, one that is surplus to requirement and so dispensed with. The modern term is dumped, I believe.

SHILPIT

Shilpit is a Scots word meaning thin and puny. The *shilpit* look is not a good look, especially if you are a man. Nowadays many men spend a lot of time, money and effort in gyms in an attempt to get rid of the *shilpit* look by building up their abs and achieving the six-pack look.

The *shilpit* look, however, is absolutely fine, and, indeed, encouraged, if you are female and relatively young. It is a look particularly sought-after by those who dream of walking down the catwalk. However, the actual word *shilpit* is not used in this case. It does not sound nearly glamorous enough to play a part in such a world.

Shilpit now is mostly used with reference to people who are lacking in physical stature, but it can also be used of people who lack courage or boldness. A timid or cowardly person can be described as *shilpit*. Who can blame the physically *shilpit* if they leave the heroics to the big guys?

The word *shilpit* can also be used to refer to liquids which, like *shilpit* people, have not much body. Thus, wine which is thin and rather tasteless can be described as *shilpit*. A liquid which is sour or bitter or lacks freshness, such as milk beyond its use-by-date, can also be said to be *shilpit*. In both of these meanings *shilpit* bears a resemblance to the word **wersh**.

People who are particularly *shilpit* often have rather sharp, drawn features and this could have some connection with the derivation of the word. The origin is uncertain, but *shilpit* may be an altered from of *shirpit* which means thin and shrunken with drawn features. *Shirpit*, in turn, may have its origins in *shairp* or *sherp*, Scots equivalents of English *sharp*.

The word *shilpit* is often used as an insult. If you want to be even more insulting you can describe someone as a *shilpit wee* **nyaff**.

SHOOGLY

I was in a cheap and cheerful café recently and sat down at a decidedly *shoogly* table. The café was very busy and understaffed and so there was little point in trying to attract anyone's attention to the problem. In any case, since the café was in central London, the word *shoogly* would not have meant very much to any of the staff. Instead, I resorted to the time-honoured, and often largely unsuccessful, method of putting a small piece of folded paper under the *shoogly* table leg.

Shoogly, which has the alternative form *shooglie* and pronounced as it is spelt, is one of the many Scots words that are so appropriate to their contexts that they are difficult to translate into English. With reference to something such as a table or chair, the word *wobbly* is often used as the equivalent of *shoogly*, although this suggests something jelly-like to me.

Wobbly was the adjective that some Londoners applied to the Millennium Bridge opened in June 2000. The Wobbly Bridge was so called because, very soon after the opening, the bridge was found to sway disturbingly as people walked over it. *Shoogly Bridge* would have been a much more descriptive expression, but, whatever you like to call it, the bridge was closed for nearly two years to allow experts to cure the *shoogle*. The adjective *shoogly* is often used of vehicles or of a journey in one of these.

Thus, a bus that is long past its prime can be a bit *shoogly* as it jolts along. A boat trip can be *shoogly*, especially when the sea is a bit rough, and old-fashioned trams seem often to have been described as *shoogly*. Apparently, journeys in a modern-style tram are more likely to be *shoogle-free*.

Shoogly can also be used to refer to people. Someone who has been ill for a while and is just trying to get around again may well be a bit *shoogly* on their legs, as can someone who is frail and elderly. In this context *shoogly* might be translated as shaky, unsteady or tottering.

Shoogly is derived from the verb *shoogle*, which has the alternative, but now less common, form *shoggle*. *Shoogle* can mean to shake, sway or rock from side to side. For example, the caravan in front of you can *shoogle* alarmingly as the driver of the car pulling it tries to negotiate unfamiliar narrow roads at too great a speed.

The verb *shoogle* is often used to describe the rocking of a baby. In an effort to pacify him or her you can *shoogle* the pram or cradle where the baby lies, or you can shoogle the baby in your arms. You can *shoogle* a baby to sleep, but *shoogle* can also mean to shake, nudge or jolt and so you can *shoogle* someone awake. To shake hands can be known as *shoogle* hands (or *hauns*).

Shoogle can also act as a noun with meanings corresponding to the verb, such as push, shake or jolt. Thus, you can give a pram a *shoogle*, give the ketchup bottle a *shoogle* (and watch the contents come gushing out to drown your food) and give your door key a bit of a *shoogle* if it fails to work first time.

As for derivation, the verb *shoogle* comes from an earlier verb *shog* which shares several of *shoogle's* senses. *Shog* has its origins in Middle English.

A grim, and all too topical, note to end on. If someone's *jaicket* (jacket) *is on a shoogly nail* , they should run for the hills or at least hide behind their desk. It means that they may well be facing redundancy.

SKEICH

Every week I seem to get more and more unsolicited mail. Added to this week's assortment was an ultra-early communication from a restaurant advertising its Christmas menu and urging me to book as soon as possible, although it is only the beginning of September. My heart sank. This was not only because I like to keep thoughts of Christmas at bay as long as possible, but also because I was reminded vividly of the horror of the staff

Favourite Scots Words

Christmas lunch. The staff Christmas lunch can be a very enjoyable occasion if you are taking part in it. However, it can be a nightmarish occasion for those who are not members of the staff, but who have to witness it and listen to it in a restaurant.

This is particularly true if those taking part in a staff Christmas lunch at a table near you are *skeich* females. *Skeich* in this sense is a Scots word meaning excited, frisky or particularly high-spirited. In the context of the staff Christmas lunch, the high spirits are often partly the result of a few glasses of some kind of alcohol.

I am not usually given to disloyalty to the members of my own sex but I have to admit that a party of females can be the worst offenders on the annoying staff Christmas lunch scene. When in *skeich* mood the levels of their voices tend to rise alarmingly and they shriek and screech at each other to the endangerment of the eardrums of the other lunchers.

The *ch* in skeich is pronounced like the *ch* in "loch" and the word skeich rhymes with the much better known Scots word *dreich*. *Skeich* has equine origins, being used of horses before it was applied to people. When referring to horses, the word has much the same meaning as it does when it is used of people. Horses, too, can be excited, frisky or high-spirited, but when they are in this state they tend just to gallop frantically round fields rather than screech at each other over lunch.

Admittedly, if a horse is *skeich* it can be bad news for someone riding it, especially if they are trying to get it to jump over a fence. A *skeich* horse can be one which is easily startled or inclined to shy. The word *skeich* can also be a verb and this, too, has equine connections. If a horse *skeichs* it shies at something or turns aside from something in fright or excitement.

The use of *skeich* is not restricted to females in the human world or to horses in the animal world. For example, children of both sexes can get a bit *skeich* before a birthday treat or cattle can suddenly get *skeich* and start kicking up their heels around a field.

In origin, *skeich* is thought to be connected with the Old English word *sceoh* meaning shy and it may be related to the Norwegian and Swedish word *skygg* meaning timid or inclined to shy.

There are few things that are quite as queer as language and the adjective *skeich*, when used of women, can have a completely different meaning from the one described above. Instead of meaning frisky and high-spirited, it can mean shy, coy, disdainful or haughty. Should you find yourself sitting next to a large group of *skeich* females tucking into a staff Christmas lunch, pray that they are *skeich* in this second sense. You will have a much more peaceful lunch.

SKELF

Scots words are often much better at conveying their meaning than their English counterparts. Take *skelf*, for example--not literally of course. A *skelf* is to be avoided at all costs.

A *skelf* is a short, sharp word for a short, sharp thing that makes you give a short, sharp yelp of pain. It is a small thin piece of wood that, quite literally, gets right under your skin. Its English equivalent is *splinter* which is not nearly so descriptive.

The *skelf* is particularly common in childhood. Children are much more likely than adults to indulge in pursuits that lead them to be attacked by *skelfs*. They tend to do things like run their hands along fences or walls as they walk along, or climb trees.

I wondered if today's ultra-protected children were less likely to fall foul of *skelfs* than those of yesteryear. However, apparently today's fad for sanded wooden floors has led to an increase of *skelfs* in the feet. This is particularly true of floors sanded by the enthusiastic, but inexperienced, DIY amateur. These often end up more *skelfy* (for *skelf* has its very own adjective) than smooth.

A *skelf* can be applied to a person. In this sense, the word does not apply, as you might think, to someone who is a right pain, but to someone who is very small and thin, and consequently weak. It is mostly used insultingly, often by macho men. Thus, you will not found find Scots fashionistas using *skelf* to describe their size zero models (although *skelf* is an apt term for them).

I was told recently that someone had come across *skelf* used as a term of endearment. I can think of nothing less endearing than a *skelf*.

Skitter *see under* **Scutter**.

Favourite Scots Words

SKOOSH

Whatever happened to the *smirr* that was formerly as regular a part of the Scottish summer as midgies? Now the *smirr*, a Scots word meaning fine rain or drizzle, has been replaced by regular bouts of teeming rain coming down in stair rods reminiscent of monsoons.

I suppose climate change will be held responsible for this. Whatever the reason, there seems to have been water, water everywhere for weeks now. Rainwater has been *skooshing* down the gutters, often ending up in great puddles when the drains cannot cope.

You can probably guess from the context what the Scots verb *skoosh* means. When applied to water, it means to gush or spurt out. The word *skoosh*, which has the alternative form *scoosh*, imitates the sound of water engaged in this activity and so is onomatopoeic in origin.

Apparently, *skoosh* did not make a written appearance in Scots until quite late on in the nineteenth century, but it sounds like the kind of word that might have been used orally for a while before being committed to paper. In fact, I am not sure how they coped without it

As to its use, if you suddenly develop a faulty kitchen tap which refuses to be turned off you may well find water *skooshing* uncontrollably all over the place. Liquids, other than water can also be said to *skoosh*. For example, if you cut yourself very badly with an ultra-sharp kitchen knife or, worse, if someone stabs you, you may well see your blood *skooshing* out of the wound as you frantically try to locate the first-aid box– or reach the phone to dial for emergency help.

On a lighter note, if a bottle of fizzy drink, whether soft or alcoholic, has been shaken over-vigorously, its contents are liable to *skoosh* over the shaker and anyone else in the near vicinity.

Solid objects can also be said to *skoosh* under certain circumstances. Sometimes water or other liquid is involved, but a certain degree of speed and a swishing sound are usually present. It has been a common part of the Scottish summer experience to date to have cars and buses *skooshing* past you as you wait at a bus stop and get drenched by the water the vehicles throw up. Should you escape to a café to dry out you will probably hear the coffee machine *skooshing* noisily away in the background. Children and *skooshing* commonly go together. You will see the young merrily *skooshing* down the slides in play parks and you will have to take smart evasive action when they skoosh round corners on their skate boards, or scooters.

Skoosh can also mean to squirt something at someone or something. Thus, children can *skoosh* water from water pistols at each other. People often *skoosh* flies, wasps and the like with some form of insecticide, although more sensitive souls take the trouble to remove them from their plate of food or jar of jam and place them outside so that they can fly in again. A spray used for this purpose, or, indeed, for other purposes, is known as a *skoosher*.

Skoosh can also act as a noun meaning a splash, spurt or jet of water, or other liquid. For example, you can borrow a *skoosh* of perfume from your friend, but it would be as well to get her permission first in case she smells the evidence on you. Or you may need to apply another *skoosh* of sunscreen to your child, if you are somewhere sunny. You may well add a *skoosh* of tonic water to your pre-dinner gin or a *skoosh* of water to your whisky. Some may even add a *skoosh* of lemonade to whisky, although hopefully not if the whisky in question is a good malt. Such a habit has resulted in a fizzy soft drink, such as lemonade, becoming known as *skoosh*.

Skoosh as a noun has a meaning unrelated to water. It can be used to refer to something that is very easy to do or deal with. Thus, a student might claim to have found the end-of-year exams a skoosh, although it would be as well to wait until after the results are out before voicing such a claim out loud. As you might expect, *skoosh* is often to be found in the world of sport. To *skoosh* it is to trounce the opposition. That is the aim of all teams everywhere.

SMEDDUM

Smeddum is a very positive word. Indeed, in modern jargon, it could be described as proactive. It means backbone, strength of character, mettle, determination, drive, energy and spirit, all those qualities that make a person actually do something, rather than just sit around thinking about it or talking about it. It can also mean resourcefulness and common sense, that markedly uncommon characteristic.

Some people who use the word nowadays frequently do so in criticism of today's way of life. In these days of ubiquitous counselling they feel that

Favourite Scots Words

we should all be reminded of the importance of *smeddum* and encouraged to sort things out ourselves. When the going gets tough the tough rely on their *smeddum*.

Many Scots words sound completely different from English words. Not so *smeddum*. It sounds as though it could quite easily be Standard English. This is not the case, although *smeddum* is descended from Old English.

Originally *smeddum* was used to refer to a fine powder, particularly finely milled meal or crushed malt put through a sieve and then used in baking. *Smeddum* was also used to describe a powder used in medicine and *red smeddum* was used as an insecticide. Robert Burns refers to this in *To a Louse*, a poem in which he satirically castigates the louse for daring to leap around a fine lady's bonnet in church.

From its powdery beginnings *smeddum* then went on to refer to the pith or essential essence of something, the central or most important part. From there it was but a short step to its modern meaning.

Those who are entirely lacking in the virtues suggested by the word *smeddum* can be said to be *smeddumless*. Actually, this sounds a bit less damning than *spineless*.

Smirr isee under **Skoosh.**

SMOUT

As a nation we tend not to wear our hearts on our sleeves or to give rein to outpourings of admiration. So it is that our language tends to be more suited to directing insults, rather than compliments, at people. As is the case with other languages, such insults are often based on the physical appearance of the target of the insult. If you are not Mr or Ms Average in appearance then you could be in trouble.

Several such insults refer to the fact that the person they are aimed at is considered to be particularly small in stature. Perhaps this is because it is assumed that small people will not have the strength to fight back, if words should come to blows. Of course this is not always the case. A lack of height is not necessarily accompanied by a lack of muscle and strength. Strong stuff can come in small bulk. A person who is considered to be lacking in physical stature, usually with an accompanying air of puniness or insignificance, in Scots is known as a *smout*. The word has the alternative spelling *smowt* and is pronounced to rhyme with English "bout". *Smout* has given rise to the adjective *smouty* meaning insignificant, of very little importance.

For some reason the word *smout* is often thought not to be effective enough on its own. It seems to require extra emphasis to make its point and so is often preceded by the word *wee*, as in "Who does that wee smout think he is?" or "Imagine a wee smout like that wanting to play rugby!" or "What on earth made her marry a wee smout like him?"

Smout has rather a fishy background, not in the idiomatic sense of slightly suspect, but in the literal sense. In fact, *smout* has clear-cut connections with a kind of fish particularly associated with Scotland, the salmon.

I am not sure how much you know, or want to know, about salmon. Very likely your interest in it only comes alive when it is presented on a plate, either in fresh or smoked form, accompanied by a slice of lemon or a dollop of mayonnaise. It may, therefore, surprise some of you to know that the salmon is of linguistic, as well as culinary, interest.

This linguistic interest is related to the salmon's rather adventurous life cycle. Salmon are described as *anadromous* owing to the fact that they are born in fresh water, migrate to the sea and then move back to fresh water. During the course of this migratory life they acquire a few labels to refer to their stage of development.

In the early stages of its development, when it is still living in its native stretch of fresh water, the salmon is known as a *parr*. When the parr matures enough to leave its fresh water habitat and make for the sea, it develops silvery scales and changes its name to *smolt*. Later, when the mature Atlantic salmon returns to its native fresh waters, it takes the name of *grilse*.

You will have observed that the fish in the middle in the above description is *smolt* and it is there that we have the origin of *smout*. *Smolt* itself is of uncertain origin, although it may have its roots in Old English. The word may be related to English *smelt*, a type of silvery sea or freshwater fish.

As indicated above, a *smout* is now used to refer to a small insignificant person, but it can also be used of a small child. Apparently, a crowd of small children can be described as a *smoutrie*. This is a great word. I must try it out on the grandchildren.

SNASTERS

As is the case with several Scots words, it is difficult to translate *snasters*. Something like confectionery or goodies might fill the bill, although, unlike these, *snasters* is usually used in a disapproving way. It refers to sugary, high-calorie things like cakes, pastries and sweets that may taste good, but rot the teeth and pile on the pounds. *Snasters* are now totally banned from most school lunch boxes.

Snasters was a word commonly used by my father in my childhood, usually in warnings not to eat too many *snasters* or I would not be able to eat a proper meal at the appointed time. It was not a word that I encountered elsewhere and for years I assumed it was derived from a Gaelic word. Although my father was not actually a Gaelic speaker, there was a distinct Gaelic influence in his speech, because both his parents were Gaelic speakers.

When I finally located a written source for *snasters*, I discovered that it was not Gaelic in origin and, in fact, that its first spelling is not *snasters*, but *snashters*. I find this very difficult to say. It tends to come out as 'shnashters' and sounds as though I have ill-fitting teeth or have had a few too many drinks. So I am sticking to *snasters*, which is an alternative spelling.

Snasters, or even more likely, *snashters*, sounds as though it is related to the Scots verb *snash*, which means to bite or snap and *snasters/snashters* are likely to have Swedish, rather than Gaelic, connections. Swedish has *snask* meaning sweets and *snaska* meaning to suck sweets.

I am not acquainted with anyone else who uses the word *snasters*, but I am sure that there must be someone out there who does.

SNELL

Scotland has very varied weather and so it is no surprise that Scots has quite a few weather words in its vocabulary. One of the Scots words that is most evocative of winter is *snell*. Like many Scots words, *snell* is also found in northern parts of England.

Snell, pronounced as it is spelt, means intensely cold. It is usually translated as bitterly cold, but *snell* is so cold that it is virtually untranslatable. The word conveys a penetrating, piercing cold that invades your very bones.

We get *snell* days and nights, we get *snell* weather and we get *snell* showers and *snell* snow. *Snell,* however, is particularly associated with wind and a sharp, biting wind it is. No barrier can keep it out. Burns comments on such winds in *To a Mouse*:

> *An bleak December's winds ensuin'*
>
> *Baith snell and keen.*

Snell is now mostly associated with weather, but it can be used of people or their manner or speech. A *snell* person is stern, severe and unbending. *Snell* remarks are caustic or sarcastic and someone for whom making such remarks is a way of life can be said to be *snell-gabbit* or *snell-tongued*.

A blow, whether literal or figurative, can be *snell*. So if someone hits you hard with a blunt object the blow can be described as *snell*. Similarly, if fortune delivers you a particularly severe piece of bad luck, that blow can also be described as *snell*.

Snell is associated with three of the senses. It can be used of taste to mean sharp or pungent. Thus, you might have a liking for *snell* cheese or *snell* sauces. Applied to smell, it can mean sharp or acrid and so smoke might be described as *snell*. *Snell* can be used with relevance to hearing or sound, meaning clear or high-pitched.

Snell once was used to mean quick, nimble or active. It was also applied to a person who was particularly sharp, quick-witted or clever. These meanings are in keeping with the origin of *snell* which is Old English *snell*, meaning swift or active.

Snell is related to German *schnell,* an adjective and adverb meaning quick or swift. As aficionados of old war movies might know, it can also be used as an interjection to encourage people to get a move on. People who are being buffeted by *snell* winds will need no such encouragement.

SONSIE

I have referred at **hurdies** to the linguistic problems of those who are invited to deliver the *Address to a Haggis* at Burns Suppers. The poem is full of words that those who are not very familiar with the Scots language might find baffling. Very early on in the poem they will encounter the

Favourite Scots Words

word *sonsie*. Nowadays, the Scots *sonsie*, pronounced as it is spelt and with the emphasis on the first syllable, is usually found in one of two related meanings. It can be used to mean *plump*, but pleasantly or attractively plump, rather than plump carrying the subtext "you need to diet right away". In this sense it is usually used with reference to women or children.

Sonsie can also be used to mean simply attractive without any reference to shape, probably a throwback to the days before the stick-insect look became popular. Again, it is mostly used to refer to women.

Now the haggis, despite the Bard's eulogy to it, cannot be said to be a particularly attractive dish to look at, although the *neeps* (turnips) and *tatties* (potatoes) add a bit more aesthetic appeal to it. The haggis can, however, correctly be described as pleasantly plump, particularly if you are serving a haggis of a reasonable size, but was it this meaning Burns had in mind?

Apparently not. *Sonsie*, like many words, has had a number of changes of meaning over the years. At one point, in the eighteenth century, it came to be a general term of approval used to describe something with a quality that appealed to the user of the word. It was possibly this sense in which Burns was using it in his *Address to a Haggis:*.

> Fair fa yir honest sonsie face,
>
> Great chieftain o the puddin race.

Usually *sonsie* in the *Address to a Haggis* is translated as jolly, cheery or cheerful, though the haggis in the address had little to be cheerful about. It was just about to be split open by a knife.

Sonsie in its plump meaning extended this sense to mean ample or substantial, as in a *sonsie* helping of food. It can also mean roomy or capacious, as in "a *sonsie*, comfortable couch" or hefty or weighty, as in "a *sonsie* blow to the head".

Sonsie then spread its linguistic wings even further and came to mean sensible or shrewd, when used of people. When used of animals, it can mean easily managed, tractable, as in "a *sonsie* breed of dog".

The original meaning of *sonsie* meant lucky, the adjective being formed from the noun *sonse* meaning good luck or prosperity.

The word *sonse* has its origin in the Gaelic word *sonas*, also meaning good luck or prosperity. *Sonse* can also mean abundance or plenty and is found in the phrase *sonse fa ye*, used to wish someone good luck or to give a blessing to them.

I quite like this phrase. Sonse fa ye!

SQUINT

Most of us acknowledge, some with some reluctance, that we have to avoid using Scots words when talking to non-Scots if we are to be understood. The problem is that we do not always recognize that a particular word is Scots. Take, for example, the word *squint*.

I am thinking of *squint* in its meaning of "not straight". If you refer to a picture on a wall as being *squint*, or if you describe a line you have just drawn as *squint*, you might well not be understood by someone with no knowledge of Scots. Even if you are understood, it could be that the person concerned has simply guessed what you mean. In English this sense of *squint* is replaced by words such as crooked, askew, on the slant as well as not straight or not level.

English does have the word *squint*, but it is restricted to situations referring to the eye. These include *squint* in the sense of an eye condition in which each eye looks in a different direction, called *strabismus* by medics. Also included is *squint* in the sense of keeping your eyes partly shut, as when you are in strong sunlight, and *squint* in the sense of a quick look, as in have a *squint* at the football results in your neighbour's newspaper.

Squint in the sense of not straight used to be found in English, but this faded from the scene. Recently, however, I thought it might be trying to make a bit of a comeback. It appears in some English dictionaries, not labelled as *Scots*, but simply labelled as *informal*. This puzzled me, as a fairly extensive straw poll which I conducted revealed a lack of knowledge of this sense of *squint* in a wide range of people in England.

I wondered if the word's inclusion in the dictionaries could have anything to do with the fact that a significant number of people who work on dictionaries are Scots. This is partly because, until recently, Scotland was home to two major dictionary companies, Chambers and Collins, and many lexicographers, who may have moved elsewhere, were trained here. (Sadly Chambers has now moved to London.) A very helpful representative of Harper Collins researched the matter for me and came to the conclusion that the failure to mark this sense of *squint* as Scots in dictionaries was simply a mistake on the part of lexicographers. This meaning is still Scots. Perhaps the lexicographers did not realize it was Scots. Perhaps it was a cunning scheme to bring to a wider audience a useful Scottish word.

STECHIE

One of the unfortunate consequences of growing older is that the joints get a bit stiff and we get a good deal less supple. You may once have been gazelle-like in your movements, but no more. Now you tend to lumber rather than skip about.

Scots has a great word to describe this condition, *stechie*. If you are *stechie* you are stiff-jointed and consequently slow-moving when any kind of physical effort is called for, even just getting out of a chair. Note that the *ch* of *stechie* is pronounced like that of "loch". *Stechie* does not rhyme with English "tetchy".

Stechie is an adjective, but it is often used as a noun to address someone who is making heavy weather of climbing a hill, going upstairs or just climbing on a bus, as in "Come on *stechie*. Get a move on." Do not be upset if someone makes such a remark to you. It may sound a bit insulting, but it is often used in a friendly, humorous way, sometimes to children or dogs.

The person so addressed need not be particularly stiff-jointed, but may be someone who easily gets out of breath, possibly from lack of exercise. Alternatively, they may be either too overweight or too lazy to be able to leap about lithely.

Indeed, *stechie* may have originally meant fat or easily made breathless, either of these states tending to make people slow-moving. Figuratively, the word can be used to mean stiff in the sense of restrained and not all relaxed, as in "We were all strangers each other and the atmosphere was right *stechie* to begin with."

Stechie probably has its roots in the verb *stech*, which has several meanings. It can mean to stuff yourself with a great deal of food, as many of us tend to do over the Christmas period. Another meaning is to stink out a place with fumes or bad air, as smokers used to do before they were banned from doing so in public places. Yet another sense refers to cramming too many people into a place. One result of this is that the people become *steched*. In other words they feel too hot and sweaty. This condition is often a result of people having too many clothes on for the temperature of their surroundings. We have all been there. You are all wrapped up for a freezing winter's day and you have to stagger round department stores in sauna-like temperatures, *steched*.

The last meaning of *stech* is the one most relevant to *stechie*, to gasp or pant as a result of over-eating or of over-exertion. In fact, in this sense it means much the same as another Scots word that it rhymes with, **pech**. If you are feeling particularly over-exerted you might do both of these, *stech* and *pech*.

Surprisingly, *stech* appears in a phrase that means the very opposite of exerting yourself. The phrase is *stech in bed* and it means to pamper yourself by having a lie-in. You may well have to do this after *steching yourself* on a feast of rich food and drink. Further effort may be beyond you.

STOOSHIE

Stooshie, whose spelling indicates its pronunciation, means an uproar, a commotion, a fuss, a row or a brawl. It is often used in connection with protest. In this context it is often attached to the verb raise or the verb create.

People can create a *stushie* about anything that displeases them, from the major to the trivial. *Stushies* have been created about suggested extensions to motorways, traffic congestion, changes to bus timetables, closure of schools in bad weather, dogs barking, dogs fouling footpaths, neighbours parking their car in front of someone else's bit of street and so on.

Stooshie is still quite commonly used in Scotland and is even found being used with reference to the august Scottish parliament where, as is the case with many national assemblies, disagreement and rows are often the order of the day. However, *stooshie* has not had the success that a few other words, such as **stramash**, have enjoyed when it comes to making its mark in the south. True, *stooshie* is occasionally to be found on the lips and in the writings of Scots who have emigrated south, but others there seem to have remained immune to its charms.

Why is this? The reason might come down to sound. *Stramash* has a more international ring to it. If you did not know better you might even think that it was a piece of modern slang. *Stooshie*, on the other hand, sounds distinctly homely. Then, although I am sure that *stooshie* is quite often to be found in a football context, it lacks the almost official connection that *stramash* seems to have with the game.

Stooshie is an excellent example of the Scots language's lack of a standard spelling. It is also commonly spelt *stushie*, but the problem does not end there. If you are looking for the word in some Scots dictionaries or in the online edition of the Scottish National Dictionary, you could find yourself out of luck. This is because the word is located under the entry *stashie* and given such alternative spellings as *steeshie* and *stishie*.

Stooshie follows many Scots words in being of uncertain origin. It has been suggested that the word, in the form of *stashie*, is a form of the English word *ecstasy*. Certainly, there are people who so love a good *stooshie* that they go into ecstasy when they are creating one.

The other day I came across the Australian and New Zealand word *stoush* meaning a fight or dispute. It can also be a verb meaning to fight or quarrel. Apparently the noun version can be applied to a war and World War 1 was sometimes referred to as the *Big Stoush*.

Several dictionaries indicate that the origin of the Australian word is unknown. But surely it must bear some relationship to *stooshie*. If so, then *stooshie* has probably been even more successful than *stramash* when it comes to infiltrating countries overseas.

STRAMASH

Sadly, a great many of our Scots words are dying out as generation succeeds generation and we all become globalized. Some words are hanging on by a thread and might well virtually disappear with the demise of the current oldest generation. But the picture is not all gloom.

Some Scots words have shown an admirable tenacity and are still in quite regular use. One of these is *stramash*, pronounced with the emphasis on the second syllable. *Stramash* is usually translated as a disorderly commotion or something along those lines.

The basic ingredients of a *stramash* are confusion and noise, usually accompanied by a crowd of people, some anger or violence and, often, a generous consumption of alcohol. Near English equivalents of *stramash* include rumpus, free-for-all and the more literary melee.

Stramash has not only demonstrated powers of endurance in its own country, but it is even to be found occasionally across the territory of our English neigbours. Now, it is hardly surprising that *stramash*, like so many other words, is to be found in the north of England. Indeed, the word appears to have been first recorded in Yorkshire dialect in the late eighteenth century.

However, *stramash* appears to have penetrated further south. Various commentators say that *stramash* is particularly common in football circles. I can only take their word for it, but this would certainly account for its popularity. Certainly, the essential ingredients for a *stramash*, as outlined above, are often present in football matches.

The origin of *stramash* is unknown and, as in many such cases, there have been various suggested etymologies. One suggestion is that, like *smash*, the word is onomatopoeic and, indeed, that *stramash* may be an intensive form of *smash*. Another suggestion is that the word may have been derived from Old French *escarmoche*, meaning a skirmish.

It could be that *stramash* has survived and extended its range of influence because it sounds like such an apt word for the situation. It conjures up thoughts of smashes and crashes. Indeed, the original Yorkshire meaning was smash and this was retained in Scots. It extended its sense to mean mishap, accident, crash or disaster and then a state of ruin or dilapidation. This might be an appropriate meaning for these recessionary times when so many businesses are likely to run the risk of ending in a *stramash*.

Stramash can also act as a verb, although it is not nearly as common as the noun form. If people *stramash* they get rowdy and create a disturbance. Back to football again. If something or someone *stramashes* you, you get thrown into a state of confusion or agitation.

Strabush is an alternative form of *stramash*. It sounds too pleasant a word to consort with rowdy crowds. No wonder it has faded from use.

STRAVAIG

Recently some of my Scots contemporaries and I were reminiscing about Scots words heard in our youth and regretting the passing of some of them. In time we got round to talking about our favourite Scots words. Undoubtedly, one of mine is *stravaig*.

I like the sound of the word. There is something airy and carefree about it and these qualities are reflected in the meaning of the word. *Stravaig*, pronounced with the emphasis on the second syllable which is pronounced like "vague", means to roam or wander around, often for pleasure and frequently with no particular destination or aim in mind.

The notion of wandering around, going where the fancy takes us, is particularly attractive to many of us in this day and age when we are chained to desks and computers for most of the week and attending to domestic chores for the rest of it. Some of us do go *stravaigin* in the country when we are released from the daily grind, but, for many, this remains a romantic notion. In any case, it is less arduous to spend a day under the duvet fantasizing about going roaming than actually to go rambling through the countryside.

Stravaig can also mean to go up and down a place and this action sometimes does have an aim. For example, members of a family might spend hours *stravaigin* the streets looking for a lost dog or you can spend ages *stravaigin* a place looking for a street name or house number that does not seem to be where it should be.

Many people use the word *stravaig* approvingly, but this is not always the case. Ramblers may love to *stravaig* across the country, but farmers and landowners do not always share their enthusiasm. If they use the word *stravaig*, they often do so in censorious tones. For farmers, *stravaigin* can suggest gates left open, livestock running loose or crops trampled. For some landowners *stravaigin*, if they have heard of the word, can suggest supposed interference with their precious privacy or seclusion. For worried parents, young people *stravaigin* the streets suggests trouble.

You will find car drivers accusing pedestrians of *stravaigin* when they cross the street while the pedestrian crossing lights are red. Incidentally, you rarely find people with children *stravaigin* in this way because children generally are sticklers for waiting for the green man to come on before they cross the street.

Stravaigers mostly do their *stravaigin* on foot, but *stravaigers* can also turn to other forms of getting around. The word has been applied to the many Scots who travelled from these shores to foreign parts as explorers, missionaries, engineers, mercenaries, etc. The *stravaigin* of the likes of Mungo Park and David Livingstone was far from aimless. The word *stravaig* made its appearance in Scots in the later part of the eighteenth century. It is thought to have its roots in an obsolete Scots word *extravage* meaning to wander about or to digress, when used of speech. This, in turn, is derived from Latin *extravagare* meaning to wander or to go beyond limits. This is related to the English word *extravagant*.

As I write this it is a sunny, crisp autumnal day, perfect weather for a *stravaig* in the country. Alas, I am chained to my computer. I will have to make do with opening a window to enjoy the fresh air.

SUMPH

English has a great many words for a stupid person. It has, for example, fool, idiot, nitwit, numskull, nincompoop, dolt, dope, clot, twit and airhead. Scots, however, can trump all of these with *sumph* which is pronounced to rhyme with "bumf".

One dictionary states that *sumph* is used mostly of men. Could this suggest that fools or nitwits are mainly men? Surely not. That would be sexist. In any case, there must be female fools in existence because *sumph* used to have the feminine form *sumphess*. Sadly, because I quite like it, *sumphess* has vanished from use.

As well as referring to a stupid person or to someone who is generally useless, *sumph* can be used to mean a surly or sullen person. This use seems to me to be particularly descriptive.

Sumph, which is of uncertain origin, can also act as a verb, although this use is not now nearly as common as the noun use. The verb means to act in a foolish, stupid way without thinking ahead. It can also mean to loaf or lie about doing nothing, or to be in a sullen sulk. Basically, the verb describes the way *sumphish* or *sumphy* people are likely to act.

Sumph is enough of an insult on its own, but often users feel the need to add an adjective to it for emphasis. They often refer to a great *sumph*, a big *sumph* or a *muckle sumph*, these expressions all meaning the same. Curiously, there do not seem to be many little or wee *sumphs* around.

Most insulting of all is the expression *donnert sumph*. *Donnert* is an adjective meaning very stupid and so a *donnert sumph* is the ultimate in idiots. *Donnert* is pronounced as it is spelt with the emphasis on the first syllable and is derived from the verb *donner* meaning to daze or stun. *Donnert*, thus, literally means having been dazed or stunned.

Donnert is not joined at the hip to *sumph*. It can stand alone and is often used to describe someone who is getting on a bit and whose mind is not as sharp as it once was. *Donnert* refers to that stage in life when the senior moments get closer and closer together. It sounds kinder than many of its English equivalents such as "loopy" or "batty", and is certainly a lot less harsh than "demented".

SWITHER

Contrary to what some people assume, the Scots language is not just a dialect of English. Scots is a separate language from English with significant vocabulary differences, although both languages have their roots in Anglo-Saxon. Unfortunately, for various historical reasons over the ages, English became the dominant language in Scotland.

This dominance has meant that many Scots words have gradually gone out of common use, as generation has succeeded generation. This is a great pity, particularly since many Scots words are much better than their English equivalents at capturing a flavour of meaning.

Some words, however, have showed remarkable staying power, despite the strength of the competition. One of these is *swither*. *Swither* means to be undecided or to hesitate. Its very sound somehow manages to convey the idea of seesawing between one decision and another.

You can *swither* between accepting and refusing an invitation. You can *swither* about which party to vote for in an election, and feature in an opinion poll as a "don't-know". You can *swither* over whether to travel by plane or train.

Should you be in two minds about something, you can be said to be *in a swither* or *even in a bit of a swither*. If you are the kind of person who goes through life in a permanent state of indecision or doubt, you may well be referred to as a *swithe*r. Well, it sounds slightly more positive than a dither.

It is a compliment to *swither* that it has shown such durability. It is an even greater compliment that it has been adopted by some non-native Scots who have come to live here and who have recognized the superiority of *swither* over the hesitant English words they were wont to use before.

As is the case with many words, the origin of *swithe*r is uncertain. It has been suggested that it has Norwegian associations, and it does have rather a Scandinavian ring to it. However, etymologists are still *swithering* over it.

- T -

Tawse *see under* **Wheech.**

THIRLED

The Scots word *thirled* means bound to something or someone by very strong ties of some kind. They can be ties of duty, ties of loyalty, ties of affection, ties of family or simply ties of habit. If you are *thirled* to a particular way of thinking or course of action you find it extremely difficult to break your connection with it.

For example you may be *thirled* to a particular political party simply because all your family vote for it. When an election comes round you do not consider the issues involved or study the policies put forward. You simply vote for the party that you are *thirled* to.

Often you become a slave to something you are *thirled* to and this gives an indication of the history of the word. Historically, a *thirl* was a slave or a serf and the verb *thirl* meant to reduce to slavery. If you were *thirled* to someone you lost your freedom and had to do obey them without question. You were bound to them in servitude. *Thirl* can have the alternative spelling *thrill* and has obvious connections with English *thrall*. If you are *in thrall to* someone you are in their control.

Later, you could be *thirled* to someone, not as a result of slavery, but because of some form of obligation. Perhaps you owed them money and had mortgaged your property to them. Perhaps they had done you some favour and you felt indebted to them. In any event, they held the upper hand and you felt that you had to kowtow to them.

A common historical meaning of *thirled* had to do with grinding grain. Often a condition of the tenancy of a piece of farmland obliged the tenant to give their business to a particular mill. The tenants were said to be *thirled* to that mill. There was no scope for shopping around and this system was sometimes extended to other businesses, such as that of the blacksmith.

Then the meaning became more figurative and people could become *thirled* to something from choice rather than compulsion. Some people are so *thirled* to one restaurant in their area that they would never dream of trying any other. Others are so *thirled* to one overseas holiday resort that they go there year after year for decades. You can say that some teenagers are so *thirled* to computer games or social media sites that they hardly ever go outside.

When someone is *thirle*d to something they are under a strong compulsion. It is almost impossible to get them to change. It is not worth even trying.

THRAWN

Most of us are, at times, guilty of double standards. Often we criticize in others the very characteristics that we boast of in ourselves. Of course, we tend to use different language to describe them and us.

So, when we are refusing to go along with the suggestions or views of someone else we use complimentary language such as firm, resolute, steadfast or sticking to our guns. When an opponent is taking a similar stance we use derogatory words such as obstinate, stubborn, uncompromising, perverse or intractable. In Scots we say that our opponent is being *thrawn*.

Thrawn is pronounced as it is spelt and so rhymes with "brawn". The word is formed from the Scots verb *thraw* meaning to twist or turn, which has a connection with English *throw*. *Thrawn* can mean any of the stubborn words listed above, but its original meaning was crooked, twisted, misshapen or deformed. A tree can be *thrawn*, as can someone's arm or other part of the body. To be *thrawn-leggit* is to have a crooked leg.

Thrawn in this sense can also be used in relation to facial features, as in *thrawn-faced* or *thrawn-gabbit* (twisted mouth), but the features can be twisted as a result of pain or anger, as well as a result of injury, illness or a birth defect. By extension, *thrawn-faced* and *thrawn-gabbit* can mean surly or sullen.

In this sense the words have much in common with the Scots word **dour** which has been adopted by some English people to describe Scots whom they regard as sullen, surly and humourless. The "dour Scot" has become something of a cliché, although such a person is more common in the English imagination than in reality.

Thrawn-headed might once have meant literally with a twisted head, but it came to mean perverse or contrary and so gave us *thrawn* as we know it today. *Thrawn* is very much a Scots word, but, like many Scots words, it is also to be found in the north of England. As far as I know, it has not yet infiltrated the leafy south. They are making do with **dour**.

TOBER

Most of us have words that were familiar to us in childhood, but that have been forgotten somewhere along life's way until something reminds of us them. For me such a word is *tober*.

It was brought to my mind the other day by someone who said that he frequently uses the word tober "meaning to chastise, cut someone down to size, etc," but that he had been unable to find such a word with this meaning anywhere, despite trawling the Internet. He was left wondering whether, in fact, there is such a word or if he had dreamed it up.

I sympathiz e with him. I have frequently been through this process myself and I have added to his conclusions the possibility that somewhere along the line an older member of the family had made the word up and it had drifted down through the generations, unknown to the rest of the world.

However, the word *tober* does exist in the wider world and it is Scots. The difficulty in locating it can be ascribed to the many variations in spelling that exist in relation to Scots words, thanks to the lack of a standard spelling. I finally found *tober* as an alternative spelling to the verb *toober*.

This means to beat or thrash, as in "tober a dog for stealing a joint of meat" or "tober a youth for stealing money". This makes it much more of a physical punishment than I associate with the word, even allowing for the fact that the days of corporal punishment are long gone.

For some reason, I can only think of idioms to pinpoint the meaning of *tober*, as I remember it. The person who made the enquiry suggests "cut down to size" and this is certainly a very apt suggestion. *Tober* also suggests to me "to put someone in their place", "to bring someone into line", "to take someone down a peg or two" or "to take the wind out of someone's sails". In other words, *tober* means to make someone realise that that they are not at all as important or as clever as they think they are and that they should start behaving in a much more humble, more obedient fashion.

The suggested derivation of *tober*, or *toober*, is an odd one. It is said to be from *tabour*, also meaning to beat or thrash. This comes from English *tabor*, a drum, especially a small drum, with the extended sense of to beat on a drum. This, in turn, is derived from Old French. Thus, *tober's* antecedents are definitely associated with physical violence.

If you are still having difficulty in getting your head round the use of *tober* and are Scots, I have a suggestion that you might find helpful. The meaning of *tober* is not too far away from "to put someone's gas at a peep".

TRAUCHLED

Trauchled is one of my most favourite Scots words. This is not because it means something particularly pleasant because it certainly does not. I like it partly because of its sound, but mostly because it conveys its meaning so well that it is virtually untranslatable into English.

In order to translate *trauchled* into English satisfactorily we need a whole raft of English words and probably an extended browse through a thesaurus. Roughly speaking, to be *trauchled* is to be utterly exhausted, overburdened, overworked, and harassed, in all cases physically, mentally and, probably, emotionally. For those of you who cannot figure out the pronunciation you will not go far wrong if you pronounce the *trauch* element to rhyme with "loch".

I witnessed the personification of *trauchled* the other day. A youngish mother got on the bus I was on, or rather she staggered on. She was trying to hold a baby in one arm while folding up an enormous buggy with the other, all the while trying to stop a toddler from rampaging up the bus and hold on to her clutch of plastic bags. She looked ready to drop and well past the end of her tether. She was, indeed, *trauchled*.

Trauchled comes from the verb *trauchle* which has several meanings. *Trauchled* as we know it is from *trauchle* meaning to exhaust, perhaps from overwork or a long journey, to overburden or harass--or a mixture of all three.

Trauchle also means to trudge along slowly or very wearily, as if you were having to force yourself to keep going. Another meaning of *trauchle* is to overwork and go drudging on in a state of fatigue and harassment.

The verb *trauchle* has also given us a noun of the same form, also with various meanings. The noun *trauchle* can refer to a long and tiring walk, to fatiguing and disheartening work or to a burden or source of trouble that wears you out.

The noun can also be applied to any exhausting and arduous struggle, such as juggling the demands of work and family or, to some unfortunates, the whole journey through life. *Trauchle* can also refer to a state of permanent muddle or chaos, usually a result of someone trying to do too much. Beware multi-tasking. It can lead to a *trauchle*.

Trauchle is of uncertain origin. It has been suggested that it is Dutch in origin and that it has some connection with Flemish *tragelen* or *trakelen* meaning to walk or proceed with difficulty.

All this talk of *trauchled* and its linguistic relatives has quite tired me out. I need a lie-down.

TUMSHIE

Tumshie is a comforting winter vegetable, found in rib-sticking stews and soups as well as being a vegetable accompaniment to meat dishes. *Tumshie* is, in fact, a turnip.

Most of us think of *neep* as being the Scots word for turnip and indeed it is both the more common word and much the older word for turnip. *Tumshie* only put in an appearance in the twentieth century while *neep* is centuries older.

Tumshie is restricted to Scotland, but *neep*, which is Old English in origin, is also found as a dialectal word in Northern England. *Neep* has also infiltrated further south and overseas thanks to Burns, or rather thanks to the ubiquitous Burns Suppers held around the anniversary of his birth. *Neeps* are traditionally served with the haggis that is the central part of the meal.

A word of warning here. Many people in England do not translate the word *neep* (or probably the word *tumshie* if they knew it) as "turnip". They call it "swede". To them the flesh of a turnip is white, not yellow. When it is yellow it is a swede.

Confusing, isn't it?

The origin of tumshie is uncertain although it may be a child's word for *turmit*, yet another word for turnip. *Tumshie* is usually used in colloquial or humorous contexts and, true enough, *tumshie* does not sound like a word that is likely to be taking too seriously. Nowadays, more people are likely to use the word *tumshie* figuratively as a term of insult, rather than literally

Favourite Scots Words

as a turnip. In this context, it is one of many Scots words that are used to mean a fool or an idiot, as in "That tumshie gave me the wrong train times."

Another word used as an insult bears a great resemblance to *tumshie* and has much the same meaning. This word is *tumfie*, with the alternative spelling *tumphie*, and is of unknown origin. So you can call someone that you regard as very stupid either a *tumshie* or a *tumfie*, but they probably will not like either.

- W -

WEAN

Wean is a Scots word for child. It now tends to be associated mainly with the west of Scotland, although it was formerly more widespread. From the look of the word you might assume that it has something to do with the English verb to *wean*. This is not so, although English *wean* has obvious connections with children since it means gradually to stop feeding a baby or an animal on its mother's milk.

The Scots word *wean* does not share a pronunciation with the English verb *wean*, pronounced *ween*. Instead, it is pronounced to rhyme with "gain" (or "pain" if you don't like children). Scots *wean* is a result of the running together of two other Scots words – *wee* and *ane*.

Ane, also pronounced to rhyme with *gain*, is the equivalent of the English pronoun *one*, and *wee* needs no explanation.

It is one of our most successful words in that it has spread its influence throughout the English-speaking world. *Wee*, meaning small or tiny (yes I know I said it needed no explanation), is rather a charming, cosy word. What a pity the word has become a verb with such a close connection with urination, and it is no longer just the *weans* who use it in that way either.

Wee first came into Scots in the late-14th century as a noun in the phrase *a lytil wee* meaning "a small distance". Derived from the Old English *waeg*, a weight, *wee* did not make an appearance as an adjective until the middle of the 15th century.

Wee ane is not always shortened to *wean*. In some parts of Scotland it retains its status as two words and is pronounced accordingly. Sometimes *wee ane* becomes *wee yin*, *yin* being also used as a Scots equivalent of the pronoun one.

Like child, *wean* can be used to refer to a small young person, aged somewhere in the halcyon time between babyhood and adolescence. It can also refer to a relationship to a parent and be used to mean offspring.

Formerly *weans* were sometimes referred to as *laddie* (boy) *weans* and *lassie* (girl) *weans*, but this practice seems to have died out. Perhaps too many mistakes were being made by well-meaning adults and certainly, at a

Favourite Scots Words

quick glance, it can be difficult to tell the difference between the sexes in the first couple of years of life. Sometimes the difficulty lasts longer. Fortunately, *grandweans* or *granweans* seem to be alive and kicking.

So if *weans* are now mostly restricted to the west, what are they called in the east and other parts of Scotland? They are called *bairns*. Well, they are by some people. Mostly they go under the universal designation, *kids*.

Bairn is derived from Old English *bearn* meaning to bear children. The word appears in a popular Scots saying *We're a* (all) *Jock Tamson's bairns* meaning that we are all human beings of equal status. This is an excellent sentiment, if not quite true.

Wee *see under* **Wean.**

WERSH

Wersh is a Scots word which is often used in relation to food. It is not the kind of word that you would find on a menu because it is far from complimentary. Something described as *wersh* is unlikely to tempt the diner's appetite.

Wersh has two food meanings and this can lead to ambiguity. Usually the distinction between two meanings is obvious from a context, but this is not necessarily true of *wersh*. It can, for example, be used of soup in both its meanings.

The older of the two food meanings can be used of soup that is pretty tasteless, being decidedly lacking in flavouring or seasoning. In some cases it is almost impossible to identify what kind of soup it is meant to be.

This older meaning is quite closely related to the Middle English word *werische,* meaning insipid, from which *wersh* was formed. The other meaning, and the more modern of the two, is used to refer to food that it is unpleasantly tart or bitter. For example, you could describe soup that has lingered rather too long at the back of your fridge and developed a disagreeable sour taste as *wersh*.

Soup is by no means the only item of food or drink that can be described as *wersh*. The old (well, let us hope it is old) British way of overcooking vegetables until they turned to slops resulted in something that was decidedly *wersh* in the sense of tasteless. Flavourless sauces optimistically intended to improve the taste of fish or meat but failing lamentably to do so, can be called *wersh*. In the days before there were health scares about salt unsalted porridge was often described as *wersh* in the sense of tasteless. Flat beer also sometimes merited the term.

Cheap (or not-so-cheap but overpriced) wine, the kind that burns your throat and stomach and all parts in between, is often referred to as *wersh* in the other sense of unpleasantly sour. Salad dressings which are heavy on the cheap-quality vinegar and light on the extra-virgin olive oil can also be labelled *wersh*.

The "sour" sense of *wersh* is the more modern and said to be the more common nowadays. However, quite a few people still use the "tasteless" meaning. The ambiguity remains. All you can be certain of is that you are unlikely to find something described as *wersh* as palatable unless you have an unusual liking for the bland or the sour.

WHEECH

Times may be hard, but every time I go out for a meal the restaurant is jam-packed, no matter what day of the week it is and no matter how foul the weather is. Perhaps the diners are desperately trying to take their minds off their dismal financial situation, or perhaps they have all decided to use up their surplus cash before it swirls off into some banking black hole.

Whatever the reason, restaurateurs are understandably taking advantage of the situation and trying to accommodate as many people as possible. More of them are restricting the amount of time diners can dally over their meal by rebooking the table after a certain time, and some are encouraging waiters to *wheech* plates away even before diners have finished eating. Put your knife and fork down at your peril.

You will probably be familiar with this dining experience – but, if you are not a Scot, you may not know the word. To *wheech* in this sense is to move something away very quickly and suddenly. It is a case of now you see it, now you don't.

In origin, the word was probably intended to imitate the sound made by something moving swiftly through the air. The English word *whisk* is similar in meaning, although it does not capture the action so successfully. In *wheech*, the *ch* sound is pronounced like that of this sound in "loch". It is

Favourite Scots Words

not pronounced to rhyme with "leech". The verb *wheech* can also mean to move along very quickly. Thus, you might almost get knocked down by a child *wheeching* along the pavement on a scooter or rollerblades, or you might see the bus you should have caught *wheeching* merrily past the bus stop before you can get to it.

As a noun *wheech* can mean a sudden sweeping movement, as in removing a plate of untouched food with an angry *wheech*. It can also mean a whizzing or buzzing sound or a blow delivered with such a sound.

In the days when corporal punishment was considered perfectly acceptable in schools, the plural form *wheechs* was used to refer to a belting with the *tawse* or leather strap – a painful and unforgettable experience, as many older readers will recollect. A *wheeky-whacky day* was a day when the belt was more in use than usual. Perhaps the teacher was in a particularly intolerant mood, or perhaps the pupils were in a particularly disobedient mood. Either way, there was much belt-wielding done on a *wheeky-whacky day*.

But to revert to a much more pleasant subject, that of fine dining. Next time you go out for a meal, have a good time but do not get so involved in a conversation that you forget to eat or to keep an eye on your plate. You might just see it being *wheeched away* before you can enjoy its contents.

WHEESHT

As a parent, however calm and reasonable you plan to be, you often find yourself issuing peremptory orders. Otherwise children would probably never get to where they are supposed to be properly dressed. "Be quiet!" is a common parental order, especially when children are squabbling in the back of the car or siblings are shouting at the tops of their voices when the baby's asleep. In Scots this command becomes *wheesht*!

In origin, *wheesht* is an imitation of the sound made by someone calling for silence and so is onomatopoeic. It has the advantage of sounding more urgent than "be quiet!" or its equivalents, although it is probably no more likely to prevent the children from making a noise. *Wheesht* also conveys the anger or impatience of the speaker more forcefully and yet it is not nearly as rude as "shut up".

Wheesht is a verb, but it is usually now mostly used as a command or interjection. People might use it to call for quietness when they are trying to work. The word is also used as an interjection when you are trying to get a child to stop crying. In this sense it is the Scots equivalent of "hush!" or "shush".

You can also use *wheesht* as an interjection if you are indicating that you do not really want to talk or think about a subject which someone has raised because you find it upsetting in some way. For example you might say, "*Wheesht*! Don't mention Christmas to me! I haven't done a thing about it." or "*Wheesht!* I couldn't stand another general election!"

Wheesht can also be a noun, but it is now found mostly in the phrase *haud yer wheesht*. It means to keep quiet about something, the equivalent of "hold your tongue".

The word *wheesht* was originally spelt *whisht* and this is still an alternative spelling. *Whisht* was once found in English, but this is no longer the case, except occasionally in some dialects. It is surprising how many words the English have let go over the centuries. We should be careful not to follow their example.

- Y -

YATTER

Yatter is one of those Scots words that does not immediately suggest its nationality. For quite a while I had not realized the word was Scots, although it is a word I use reasonably frequently, especially when I am on a trainful of mobile *yatterers*. But *yatter* is definitely Scots and it makes an appearance in all the Scots dictionaries.

Yatter means to talk on seemingly endlessly about very little. The word is onomatopoeic in origin and has been coined to imitate the sound made by somebody chattering at length. It is pronounced to rhyme with "natter" and shares a similarity in meaning with it. However, *yatter* is more likely to be used in a critical way. In this respect it is more like the English word *witter*.

As indicated earlier, *yatter* can be used of people who spend journeys chattering away incessantly into their mobile phones, rather than reading, admiring the scenery or just taking some time to think. Some people are fortunate enough to be paid to *yatter* on. You must have heard them on television on occasions such as election nights-- commentators and politician rambling on while they wait for something interesting to happen.

Politicians are particularly noted for their tendency to *yatter*. It is fitting, therefore, that a website which collates and keeps us up to date with the musings and activities of politicians is was given the name *Yatterbox*.

Yatter can also be used to mean to talk loudly and unintelligibly. This use is sometimes unfair. It is quite frequently applied to people speaking animatedly in their own language, but a language that is foreign and unintelligible to the listener who describes it as *yattering*. You may hear it used when a group of people from another country are getting on a bus trying to explain to each other the complications of the local public transport system. They are often accused of *yattering* and holding up the rest of the passengers.

Yatter can also mean to nag or carp on about something. Such *yattering* is popularly assumed to be the preserve of women. If this is true, and I query the truth of it, it is often because men never listen first time round.

Not only people *yatter*. It can be used of animals. For example, dogs when yelping can be described as *yattering*. It can be used of flowing water, as in a *yattering* river, and it can be used of teeth chattering with fear, cold, etc.

Some dictionaries suggest that *yatter* is to be found in English also. Like many Scots words it is certainly likely to be found over the border in parts of northern England, but I am not convinced that it has penetrated the deep south to any great extent. A personal straw poll suggests that it has not. The dictionary entries could be a result of the fact that a large proportion of lexicographers are Scots, influenced, whether consciously or not, by their own language.

In meaning *yatter* has much in common with the modern ubiquitous phrase *yada yada yada*, or *yadda yadda yadda*, which we inherited from America. It has been suggested that this phrase has its origin in *yatter*. In fact the origin of the phrase is uncertain, but there are more plausible contenders than *yatter*, although it is possible that *yatter* had more success in America than it did in England. However, it seems much more likely that the *yada* phrase has its origins in the Jewish-American slang of the 1940s.

I am not a huge fan of *yada yada yada*, either the concept or the phrase. I much prefer the homespun *yatter*.

Copyright ©2014 Betty Kirkpatrick.

All rights reserved. No part of this publication may be reproduced, distributed, or transmitted in any form or by any means, including photocopying, recording, or other electronic or mechanical methods, without the prior written permission of the publisher.

Printed in Great Britain
by Amazon.co.uk, Ltd.,
Marston Gate.